STUDIES ON MYS...

The Court Cards

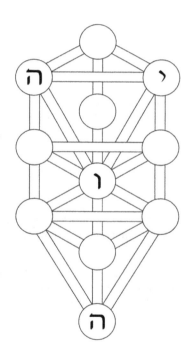

Yolanda M. Robinson, PhD

ISBN-13: 978-1484806401
ISBN-10: 1484806409

Copyright © 2013 by Yolanda M. Robinson, PhD.

All Rights Reserved. No part of this publication may be reproduced in any form or by any means without prior written authorization from the author.

Library of Congress Cataloging-in-Publication Data

LCCN: 2013908430

Robinson, Yolanda M.
  Studies on mystical tarot: the court cards / Yolanda Robinson
  1. Tarot. 2. Qabalah. 3. Rosicrucianism. 4. Golden Dawn.
  5. Transformational psychology

All images from the Builders of the Adytum Tarot deck are personal interpretations of the author. Builders of the Adytum does not endorse in any way the material contained in this work.

All images from the deck by A. E. Waite (author) and Pamela C. Smith (illustrator) are reproduced from the 1911 edition published by William Rider & Son, LTD. These pictures are in the public domain in the United States.

Design and layout by: Paul Kjell Austad

The use of Tarot for self-inquiry should in no way become a substitute for legal, financial, medical or any other professional advice

STUDIES ON MYSTICAL TAROT:
THE COURT CARDS

TABLE OF CONTENTS

A STUDY GUIDE TO THE COURT CARDS IN THE ROSICRUCIAN TRADITION

INTRODUCTION	1
WHY A WORKBOOK ON COURT CARDS?	4
THE TREE OF LIFE	6
Tree of Life with Courts	11
THE SYMBOLIC POWER OF NUMBER FOUR	12
RELATIONSHIPS AND CORRESPONDENCES	15
PLACING THE QUATERNITIES IN A GIVEN CONTEXT	17
INTERPRETING THE ENERGY OF THE COURTS TODAY IN DIVINATION SPREADS	20
SOME FINAL OBSERVATIONS	22
The Four Qabalistic Worlds as Concentric Circles on the Tree of Life	24
Summary of Correspondences	25
Zodiac Wheel with Corresponding Decanates According to BOTA and Golden Dawn	27
Major Arcana Planetary and Zodiac Alignments	28
Qabalistic Arrangement of the Courts	29
YOD	31
KING OF WANDS	33
KING OF CUPS	36
KING OF SWORDS	39
KING OF PENTACLES	42

HEH 45

QUEEN OF WANDS 47

QUEEN OF CUPS 51

QUEEN OF SWORDS 54

QUEEN OF PENTACLES 57

VAU 61

KNIGHT OF WANDS 63

KNIGHT OF CUPS 66

KNIGHT OF SWORDS 69

KNIGHT OF PENTACLES 71

FINAL HEH 75

PAGE OF WANDS 77

PAGE OF CUPS 80

PAGE OF SWORDS 83

PAGE OF PENTACLES 86

BIBLIOGRAPHY AND SUGGESTED READING 89

A STUDY GUIDE TO THE COURT CARDS IN THE ROSICRUCIAN TRADITION

Introduction

Tarot is a mystery to me. It will always be. What started as an intellectual curiosity in my mid-twenties slowly became a method of self-inquiry, and an often intrusive friend. Once we step outside the box of gathered expectations stemming from superstitious gypsy tales, exploitation movies, and carnie psychic fairs, we realize that Tarot is more than just another fortunetelling device. There is something alluring, mysterious about this pack of seventy-eight cards. We need to access their wisdom carefully, allow the cards to speak to us and connect to soul. Every single card in Tarot can act as a Gate for us to discover a hidden part of our own self. But this is a process that requires time, patience, and humility.

I started this study guide as a workbook for students at the University of Philosophical Research in Los Angeles, California, but soon realized that I needed to expand the work beyond the scope of a particular course and directly address the cards from a mystical and esoteric perspective. I make no excuses; this is the way that Tarot works for me. Older traditions find their way into our everyday life in order to help us understand that the many challenges we face are usually archetypal. Archetypes are neutral forces; they might change names and garments, but in essence they are defined by the behavioral patterns that they bring forth in all of us. And we are the ones who give archetypes their form as they constellate in our psyche and personality.

We live in an ever-increasing complex world. Yet, our ability to understand the world around us depends on how we understand ourselves. Self awareness leads to self-knowledge. Self-knowledge helps us understand others better. We are all in this together. And, you might be asking by now, how

1

STUDIES ON MYSTICAL TAROT

would sixteen court cards—out of seventy-eight cards in a deck—make a difference in my life? You might be amazed.

Welcome to the kingdom of the Courts. These sixteen cards are one of the three basic structures of a regular deck of Tarot cards: twenty-two Major Arcana and fifty-six Minor Arcana divided into four elements with ten numbered cards and four court cards each. The Courts, however, escape the mere designation of "minor" or "lesser" arcana because they represent an independent structure: a quaternary structure that links Majors and Minors while displaying for us a hierarchy of energies that can become useful tools for self-inquiry. The Courts in the system we are here studying are displayed as individuals, yet they can assume any other form because these are independent energies, principles and qualities that relate to each other in some kind of hierarchy or special order, depending on the message that their creator/artist wishes to convey.

The more we work with a good, solid deck the more that each section of the pack speaks to us directly, revealing their individual as well as group structure. Observe carefully, because each part is conveying its own interpretation of Law, its own way of expressing how cosmic forces and universal principles help us connect with our Higher Self. Hermetic work is all about personal transformation, about alignment with cosmic forces and about connecting with our own divinity.

What I like to call "traditional tarot" stems from the Renaissance and evolved through the centuries to become a mystical, esoteric and hermetic tool adopted by secret guilds and mystery schools of the western tradition. By "hermetic" I mean all the various influences that have shaped the western mind, including pre-Socratic traditions, Gnosticism, magic, Cabala, alchemy, astrology, Neoplatonism, Romanticism, and other important social and cultural trends.

Tarot is an offspring of playing cards introduced to the Hispanic Peninsula and southern Italy by the Moors. Returning Crusaders and traders also contributed to the incredible explosion of cultural exchanges between East and West that characterized the Middle Ages and gave form to the Renaissance. It is essential to keep a historical perspective when delving

The Court Cards

into Tarot, because the product that we have today, the thousands of decks available to us now, is a relatively recent phenomenon. Tarot as an esoteric tool might be a product of the XVIII and XIX centuries, but as we trace its pedigree from the late Middle Ages through the Neoplatonic schools in Florence (in particular), and in Bologna, to the royal courts in Milan and other parts of northern Italy, as well as to the Hispanic Peninsula, we cannot lose sight of the strong pedagogical and mystical overtones present in the decks from their inception.

We also need to keep in mind the vast domain covered by the Spanish and Portuguese Empires, and the cultural impact that both Jewish and Muslim traditions had for several centuries in these areas and other parts of Europe. Serious academic study of Tarot is just beginning and it is revealing to us the influence exerted by hieroglyphic, emblematic and miniature art; the role played by Cabala, the Art of Memory, the Picaresque novel, Troubadors and Chansons de Geste, to name just a few. Literature begets literature, art begets art; and human consciousness expands and adapts and adopts accordingly. Nothing is ever forgotten; it is all in the reservoir of the collective unconscious.

STUDIES ON MYSTICAL TAROT

Why a Workbook on Court Cards?

This book is meant for students who are interested in understanding Tarot within the Rosicrucian tradition, as defined by the Golden Dawn and Builders of the Adytum.

The workbook does not cover the Marseilles-style decks *per se*, although many of the observations and interpretive techniques found here could easily be applied to Marseilles decks as well as to many other decks available today.

The Courts exude a life of their own. They offer us a hierarchy with special energies contained among themselves, like a family or community or tribe. As much as we try to define them within certain given parameters (like we will attempt to do in this study), you will find them eluding our scrutiny, demanding more amplitude. The "courts" were part of playing cards before the Trumps or Major Arcana existed—before a fifth suit was added to the *trionfi* cards that later became known as *tarocchi*. At first, there were usually three royalty figures. The so-called Mamluck deck included three court cards alluding to ranks of *roy* (*rey*, *king*) and two vice-roys (*naib*; *naibi*). Eventually, human figures replaced the abstract royalty, a "queen" was added, and at one point a few more court figures and categories were included in some early decks. These royal figures walked in and out of the decks' courtyard until the ubiquitous number four finally prevailed, and we now have four royalties or "courts" per suit.

The sixteen Court Cards here presented correspond to a special mystical cosmology. The cards can be used for divination, but at the same time we must be aware of their mystical roots. The intention of the authors was to present a point of view, a system of knowledge and a school of thought. We need to honor that. I have found that careful study of these cards does open for us new levels of awareness, new ways of looking at ourselves and others. There is something uncanny and magical about the intuitive connections that we make when using cards that follow a specific esoteric tradition. The Golden Dawn and Builders of the Adytum emphasize the ritual use of Tarot images. The cards represent specific vibrations and relationships to colors and to the Tree of Life, which is the map used to gain access to our

The Court Cards

own divinity, and also a means to tap into the School of Ancient Wisdom, into the energies that "in-form" us from above as we ourselves "in-form" those below us. Mystical Tarot is all about relationships, connections, personal and cosmic imprints and their application in our daily life, for the higher good.

Some of the information and intimations in this work stem from my years of study with Builders of the Adytum. However, this book reflects my own personal interpretations, which at times might differ from BOTA's basic approach to the study of Qabalistic Tarot. My intention is to place Tarot and the Court cards here studied as energies of transformation, as alchemical tools that reflect some of the mystical ways to approach divination and self-inquiry by using Qabalah and the Tree of Life.

I am including a basic bibliography for those students interested in a deeper understanding of "Cabala" (which is the way that the Hebrew Encyclopedia spells our word Kabbalah). Esoteric studies require patience and an open mind. I invite you to expand on this work; keep a journal and write down your own impressions about the Court system here presented; see how some of the correspondences and ideas offered in this text could be transferred to the interpretations of other decks. The use of emblematic art and alchemy by Hermetic schools like Rosicrucianism was meant to evoke specific qualities and behavioral patterns in the psychic field of the practicant using the Tarot cards as agents of change.

Allow intuition to guide you and approach the Courts with a beginner's mind, like the Fool who opens the Tarot deck with open arms and with no expectations.

STUDIES ON MYSTICAL TAROT

The Tree of Life

The Rosicrucian and Golden Dawn traditions are rooted in the Cabala (*Qabalah*). The Tree of Life and the Hebrew letters become a blue print or map to guide us on our personal spiritual unfoldment. The Tree consists of ten visible *ciphers* or *Sephiroth*.

Cabala means giving and receiving. The ten divine emanations on the Tree of Life provide a master pattern for our ascent and descent through each numerical emanation or *Sephirah* in order to gain access to various levels of awareness. This awareness connects us to ancient wisdom delivered by those ahead of us on the Path of Return. As we tune into these higher levels of wisdom, we also give to those who are able to receive the radiations from us. The Breath of God as **Ruach** becomes the living breath that connects and transmits the Knowledge of the Ancients to all of us through alchemy of the soul. This is the process that helps us connect to our Higher Self.

The word *Sephiroth* means "ciphers, numerations, emanations;" each emanation or Sephirah becomes a vessel with its own energies (an alchemical vessel of transformation), with its own world, with its own qualities; giving and receiving the Divine Ruach, and opening in each of us archetypal dimensions that define our human nature, as well as our personal journey of transformation. The Limitless Light called *Ain Suph Aur* initiates the process of self-manifestation as it concentrates in the Central Point called Kether and brings forth the sequential emanations.

1. Kether, *Crown:* This is the Source, the First Whirling of Creation, the Sphere of the Limitless Light; seat of the Indivisible Self *Yekhidah;* the I AM.

2. Chokmah, *Wisdom:* As the Light recognizes itself in the two, AB the Father emanates as the *masculine* energy that seeds Creation. Chokmah is the seat of *Chaiah*, the universal Life-Force, and also of the Sphere of the Zodiac. The Hebrew letter Yod and the Atziluth World of Archetypes and Emanations are connected to Chokmah.

The Court Cards

3. Binah, *Understanding:* Sephirah assigned to Aima the fertile Mother, the feminine energy that brings forth Creation, and hence the emanations of the next seven Sephiroth across the Abyss. Saturn, with its darkness, heaviness and strictures, is assigned to this Sephirah, perhaps to remind us that Creation is the result of Consciousness contracting and collapsing unto Itself. Chokmah and Binah, like the Yin/Yang principle, are the two eternals that bring forth life. The Hebrew letter Heh and Briah, the World of Creation, are connected to this Sphere. The first three Sephiroth are called the *Supernal* or *Divine Triad.*

4. Chesed, *Mercy,* is assigned to Jupiter and represents the "limitless substance" as Majesty and Magnificence. It is an expansive and generous emanation, as it receives from the Mother and pours out her blessings. This is also the seat of cosmic memory. Regulation and Adjustment are required for this emanation to self-regulate its power. This is one of the responsibilities of the next Sephirah.

5. Geburah, *Severity,* assigned to Mars and Volition (will). This Sephirah also connects to words that relate to Justice, Law, Fear and Strength. Chesed, Geburah and Tiphareth, the next Sephirah, are a reflection of the Supernal Triad above, and are called the *Egoic Triad,* Triad of Individuality and of the Higher Mind. The powers of this Triad are concentrated in Tiphareth.

6. Tiphareth, *Beauty,* is the center of the Tree and reflects the Christ Consciousness, the "Christos" or "Anointed Consciousness" of Jesus or the Buddha. This is the Sphere of the Sun and where primal transformative energy is made available to Generic Humanity for self-realization and transformation. The six-pointed star is often associated with Tiphareth; it consists of two triangles: one going up and the other down—male and female energies forming a hexagram as symbol of spiritual harmony. It is the seat of the third letter of the Holy Tetragrammaton, Vau, and where the Yetziratic world of Formation radiates its influence to the Sephiroth of the Egoic Triad above and the Personality Triad below.

STUDIES ON MYSTICAL TAROT

7. Netzach, *Victory*, assigned to Venus. This is the sphere of Desire where all expressions of our creativity are given stimulus and full potentiality. It also reflects Chesed, the fourth Sephirah above. Netzach also reflects the "beauty" of Tiphareth as applied to our Path of Victory. It sits diagonally across Geburah, sphere of Adjustment, Severity and of the fiery Mars. The energies of Venus and Mars balance each other through the sphere of Tiphareth.

8. Hod, *Splendor*, assigned to Mercury (Hermes). This is the seat of the intellect and, as such, can teach us about the mind and its volatility, as well as its adaptability. This sphere sits below Geburah, across Netzach and diagonally from Chesed, crossing first Tiphareth. Notice how all these Sephiroth mirror, reflect and influence each other. The dynamics of these emanations helps us understand some of the meanings of the Minor Arcana and the ways that memory, volition, imagination and desire determine and give form to the world of manifestation.

9. Yesod, *Foundation*, assigned to the Sphere of the Moon. This is also the astral world of dreams, intuition, psychic energies, and automatic consciousness; as well as the "seat" of the Vital Soul permeating all of creation. Yesod provides the foundation or basis for all our actions and reactions. It is the source of Malkuth the Kingdom and also expresses our relationship to the Triads above. This Sephirah is our *Gate to Higher Consciousness* and the Portal through which we embark on our journey of self-knowledge and self-realization.

10. Malkuth, *Kingdom*, Sphere of Mother Earth, the dwelling of the Shekhinah as God's emanating presence in all creation. This is also the sphere of Kallah the Bride. It represents Assiah, the physical world of manifestation. Malkuth is placed on the Middle Pillar of the Tree of Life, aligned with Yesod, Tiphareth, and Kether. This is the Pillar that balances the Tree. The invisible Path of Daath, Knowledge, is also placed on the Middle Pillar, in the Abyss through which we connect with the Supernals. Mystically this is where all the Sephiroth converge in order to help us reach higher consciousness. It is through the work that we perform in Malkuth that we gain access to the various levels of transformation that lift our consciousness into union with

The Court Cards

the One. Tiphareth, as sphere of the Sun, will render the Light that will guide us along the way. We are meant to, eventually, arrive at the Abyss, cross the Path of Daath and fold into the Crown, into the One. Thus we fulfill the promise that, "Kether is in Malkuth and Malkuth is in Kether."

STUDIES ON MYSTICAL TAROT

#1 Kether - Crown
Limitless Spark
Primal Spark
Aces

#3 Binah - Understanding
Aima the fertile Mother
Sphere of Saturn
Threes and Queens

#2 Chokmah- Wisdom
Ab the Father
Sphere of the Zodiac
Twos and Kings

#5 Geburah - Severity
Justice, Law and Volition
Sphere of Mars
Fives

#4 Chesed - Beneficence
Mercy - Cosmic Memory
Sphere of Jupiter
Fours

#6 Tiphareth - Beauty
Christ Consciousness
Sphere of the Sun
Sixes and Knights

#8 Hod - Splendor
Intellect
Sphere of Mercury
Eights

#7 Netzach - Victory
Desire
Sphere of Venus
Sevens

#9 Yesod - Foundation
Vital Soul
Astral Body
Sphere of the Moon
Nines

#10 Malkuth - Kingdom
Earth and physical world
Tens and Pages

The Court Cards

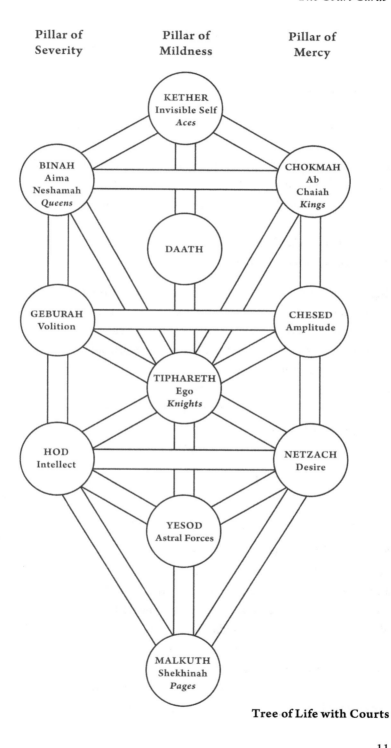

Tree of Life with Courts

STUDIES ON MYSTICAL TAROT

The Symbolic Power of Number Four

Squares and rectangles and cubes: forms that contain and that provide solidity and structure. The number four offers us the quaternary of the Courts filled with many possibilities and potentialities of interpretation. The Minor Arcana in the esoteric decks that we are here exploring consist of four suits with ten numbered cards, or pips, and four court cards. The quaternities (4 x 4) assigned to the Courts in the Rosicrucian Qabalistic tradition were intended to form a bridge between the Majors and the Minors. This bridge offers us a hierarchical system of image-concepts that reflect our relationship to power and to social structures, as well as emblematic symbols that project specific qualities and personas we either assume ourselves or encounter in others throughout daily life.

The sixteen Courts, just like the forty pips (the Minors numbered from one to ten) and the twenty-two Majors, weave a structure of mystical interconnections that relate to the four elements (Fire, Water, Air, Earth); to the four Qabalistic Worlds (*Atziluth, Briah, Yetzirah and Assiah*); to their assigned Zodiac decanates and planets; as well as to the energy of their assigned Hebrew letter in the Holy Tetragrammaton—YOD HEH VAU HEH, the revered name of God as Yahweh (or Jehovah). When we read this holy name, *from right to left*, it should be so written:

יהוה

י	ה	ו	ה
Fire	Water	Air	Earth
Yod	Heh	Vau	Heh

Yod: "hand"; "to thrust"; "coition"
Yod is the smallest letter of the Hebrew alphabet (also called the "Flame" alphabet from the Chaldean tradition); this small letter is also part of all Hebrew letters, as they spring forth from the first letter that spells "Yahweh." Yod is drawn suspended in mid-air, full of potentialities, discreet and ubiquitous. In Jewish mysticism, Yod is perceived as a flame, a sudden movement, a cosmic messenger. Yod also intimates "coitus" and the bliss of the union with the One. Yod is the spiritual energy we find in Life and signifies the cosmic Light when allowed full expression and potentiality.

Heh: "wind-door"

Heh is used like the definite article "the." The letter often serves to add special emphasis to a word, like an exclamation mark. Heh is found twice in the Holy Tetragrammaton and connotes divine revelation. It is assigned to the two "feminine" energies in Qabalistic Tarot (Water and Earth). Heh is connected to breath as a means for spiritual development and mystically represents the way that God created the entire cosmos through his breath (***Ruach***).

Vau/Vav: "nail; hook"; indefinite article and connector

Vau implies "*that which holds things together*." The letter is drawn very, very straight, like a vigilant soldier standing up in attention or like a pillar suggesting inner strength. Vau intimates righteousness, correct behavior; but also uniqueness, and the need to express who and what we really are. Vau suggests wholeness, as something contained in and of itself. It also implies the "ray of light" that God brought down into creation; therefore, it represents the conjunction which unites us to God and to our own divinity. Vau also refers here to the six Sephiroth from Chesed to Yesod, influenced by the Ego in Tiphareth, where Vau sits along with the Knights.

Final Heh: This letter as Final Heh represents Kallah the Bride, the dwelling of Shekhinah, and the world of physical manifestation. As "Breath of God" it connects to Kether and to the active and cyclic principles of creation.

The Hebrew letters, the "letters of Abraham," are meant to be meditated and gazed upon. The moment that we "gaze" at these letters and connect them to Tarot we are placing the cards into a mystical dimension all of their own. That means you can use the impressions you receive from this Qabalistic connection for personal growth, for self-analysis, for divination. We cannot forget that traditional Cabala became an essential part of the Hermetic movement inspired by the Renaissance schools; and whatever version of this tradition transformed through the years into the Qabalah embraced by such esoteric orders like the Martinists and the Rosicrucians in the 18TH and 19TH centuries, the moment that Tarot was placed within their system and linked to schools of ancient wisdom, the cards acquired more mystical dimensions. *Tarocchi* was a child of the Renaissance, already infused with mystic qual-

STUDIES ON MYSTICAL TAROT

ilities; the Golden Dawn transformed Tarot into a magical alchemical tool that would serve as a Gate to initiate aspirants into higher mysteries.

One important observation about the Four Qabalistic Worlds: The World of Emanations, Atziluth, generates the other three Worlds. Each new World carries more density as well as a descending scale of brightness. In the physical plane of Assiah, the World of Manifestation, we find the accumulation of the grosser elements and qualities of the previous three worlds. In addition, each world emanates ten Sephiroth of its own; and each Sephirah likewise. We thus end up with the concept of worlds within worlds, a holographic universe in constant expansion. Our role in this immensity is to realize that our thoughts and actions do affect the indomitable forces of creation in ways that we cannot even begin to fathom.

Relationships and Correspondences

If we look at the Holy Tetragrammaton as the mystical structure within the Minor Arcana, and if we assign to every Arcanum a dimension based on the Hebrew letter that corresponds to its Suit, its Element, and its Qabalistic world we enrich the interpretation of a divination, especially if we are reading with a Marseilles deck. The court cards are placed on the Tree of Life as follows: Kings are placed in Chokmah, *Wisdom*, Sphere of the Zodiac; Queens in Binah, *Understanding*, Sphere of Saturn; Knights are placed in Tiphareth, *Beauty*, Sphere of the Sun and seat of the Ego or Higher Self; and Pages are placed in Malkuth, *Kingdom*. This placement on the Tree adds an important level of interpretation to the Courts, because they all establish a special energetic connection to their Sephirah, as well as to the Sephiroth above and below. It is all interconnected through visible and invisible Paths.

Kings and Queens are part of the *Supernal Triad* formed by Kether / Chokmah / Binah. This is the Divine Triangle that gives creation impulse in all its dimensions as Kether, the Indivisible Self, begins the primal swirling into the Sephiroth below. The manifest universe where we dwell is the *mental* creation of the Father and the Mother. Kether activates both Chokmah and Binah, just like these two Sephiroth constantly activate and influence each other. The rest of the Sephiroth come forth out of their Union, as the contracting force of Saturn (assigned to Binah) assists the impulse through the Abyss into the fourth Sephirah, Chesed. Inside this Qabalistic configuration, the rest of the Sephiroth—from four to ten—represent aspects of human consciousness that need development or purification as we learn to ascend and descend the Tree through the various alchemical vessels that each Sephirah represents.

Shekhinah, for example, dwells in the third Sephirah as the feminine aspect of God. She also dwells in Malkuth—the tenth Sephirah—as *Kallah the Bride*. Malkuth is the Sephirah assigned to the Pages or Knaves, who happen to be the *"thrones" of the Aces*. The *"Bridegroom"* dwells in the sixth Sephirah, Tiphareth, seat of the four Knights.

STUDIES ON MYSTICAL TAROT

Queens and Pages carry the energy of the Hebrew letter Heh into different interpretive dimensions, since they reflect two different elements (Water and Earth) and two different planes (Briah and Assiah). Nevertheless, both are "feminine" elements, just like Fire and Air are considered "masculine" elements (assigned to the worlds of Atziluth and Yetzirah).

All these allusions might not be needed in a divination, but sometimes these are the subtleties that penetrate our soul and take us into higher awareness of ourselves and of the forces that surround us. When you study Qabalah and Tarot and connect to any of these correspondences while using the Courts in divination or meditation, you might need to explore the intuitive hits or resonances at a deeper level. Use your intuition because these cards are meant to work through influences exerted on our astral body, below (or above)our normal level of consciousness. Our capacity of attunement to the influences stemming from the astral plane often determines the way that we access information available to us through the power of intuition.

As noted above, the Pages and the Aces have a special relationship; this relationship could be quite useful in readings. Aces signify the "root of the powers" of the element assigned to them; their seat is in Kether the Crown, the first Sephirah and the beginning of the whirlings of creation. The Pages sit in Malkuth, the tenth and final Sephirah, and they symbolize the *full potentiality* of manifestation of their element. Aces and Pages occupy the *same Quadrant* on the Zodiac Wheel. In addition, the Pages are considered the *"thrones"* of the Aces. Making these connections could be very helpful in a divination where both Aces and Pages appear, even if they do not correspond to the same suit.

Majors, Pips and Courts can be seen as three holographic systems within a cosmology. These systems or constellations add and subtract qualities to and from each other, expanding and constantly changing *ad infinitum* the potentialities of creation, just like a magical mandala. And, as we work with all of them in divination, these three systems will complement and contradict each other, weaving associations and eliciting impressions that require we drop our logical mind and enter the world of nonsense, alchemy, magic and intuition.

Placing the Quaternities in a Given Context

How is the Primordial Fire activated in each King and how is it reflected in divination? How does this Fire affect the ruleship and domain of a King in relation to the other cards in a spread? What qualities of the element of Water would characterize each of the Queens in their ruleship? Which mystical aspect of the Hebrew letter Heh would you apply to a Page of Cups, or to a Page of Pentacles? How would the Knight of Swords (Air of Air) reflect the archetypal wisdom of the Hebrew letter Vau?

We might find ourselves asking these kinds of questions depending on the depth of a given reading, or when we use the cards for meditation. But most of the time these Qabalistic and mystical relationships are kept on the back of our mind, ready to come forth if needed and when we are ready to use them effectively. Do not force these correspondences; they are not meant to impress the querent or client; on the contrary, esoteric information might turn your clients off, and away. Sometimes too much information tends to block the free flow of intuition in a reading. If you are meant to make a Qabalistic connection it will happen whether you are looking for it or not. Do not use mystical wisdom to show off.

Are these correspondences needed when we read the cards? Not really. Like the Art of Memory, these associations are supposed to work like mnemonic devices. You will draw upon the connections when needed— when you are connected to the energies of Ancient Wisdom available to us when our psychic field is prepared accordingly. Allow the cards to impress you directly. Simplify your interpretation of the Courts at the beginning of your studies and slowly amplify their meaning. Keep a journal and trust your intuition.

The court cards are often compared to the sixteen categories of the Myers-Briggs personality test. Even though the cards adapt themselves to the various and different qualities of human behavior reflected on the Myers-Briggs, I find this classification a bit simplistic, for both the Courts and us: we are all much more complicated than that. We all carry the twelve Zodiac signs within, and each of us relates to these energies and planets not just according to our birth date but also to all the propensities imprinted in us by our socio-cultural environment.

A court card might indicate a specific person in a reading; yet, next time the same card appears it might point to a given quality in a situation, or suggest a manner or attitude to resolve a quandary. The cards do not necessarily have to connect with specific people in our life; and the archetypal energy that they exude in divination could be just as powerful as any major arcanum. Often, a specific behavioral pattern can be brought to full understanding when we associate the cards with energy patterns according to the Element, the Suit, the Zodiac placement and the Qabalistic world.

Still, we tend to look at the Courts and relate them to people. What role would a Page, for example, play in today's social structure? Pages or knaves used to be servants, slaves or foot soldiers; the *infantes*, messengers or immature energies with the least important influence in the old royal hierarchy ("connected to court but not in court"). That was before esoteric schools began to assign to the page/knave/valet new meanings and eventually transformed them into the "thrones" of the Aces and they became either androgynous or female characters. In some Egyptian style decks, for example, the knave is a slave. Compare this designation with the Golden Dawn or Aleister Crowley's Princesses, or with other newer, modern versions of the Courts. The knave card has endured many transformations through the centuries; it never ceases to intrigue us and to bring forth more and more interpretations.

Let us look at the Knights. Considered a masculine energy, the Knight carries out the mandate of the kingdom. He must exude virility and will. Let us pause here for a moment and remind ourselves that "virtue" and "virility" come from the same etymological root. How energy is depicted in the Knights will help you analyze their ability to move between the six Sephiroth assigned to the World of Yetzirah. In most decks the Knights are usually depicted riding a horse that either mirrors the character of the rider, or suggests additional dimensions for the card. The Golden Dawn Tarot places the Kings on a horse instead of a throne, and the knights are now Princes riding a chariot drawn by the emblem of the *fixed* Zodiac sign that they represent:

The Court Cards

Wands: Prince of the Chariot of Fire: Chariot drawn by a lion (the fixed sign Leo).

Cups: Prince of the Chariot of the Waters: Chariot drawn by an eagle (the fixed sign Scorpio).

Swords: Prince of the Chariot of the Winds: Chariot drawn by fairies with butterfly wings (the fixed sign Aquarius).

Pentacles: Prince of the Chariot of Earth: Chariot drawn by a bull (the fixed sign Taurus).

You might encounter Golden Dawn decks with designations that follow the *Book T*, which can be confusing because the knights are also called kings. Aleister Crowley's Thoth deck simplifies the classification and dispenses with the double names for knights and kings. The Knight is now the consort of the Queen and ruler of the kingdom. Crowley's classification is Knight/ Queen/Prince/Princess.

Interpreting the Energy of the Courts Today in Divination Spreads

How would the Air element reflected through the image-concept of a king be used today to implement a mandate, or to supervise an industry, a government office, or to help us resolve a challenge? Would a "fiery" king with ruleship of the subconscious waters of emotion and creativity be more effective in dealing with a home-related problem than an airy, brainy king with a sword? What kind of action or resolution could be suggested in a reading by the Knight of Pentacles versus the Page of Cups? Which of the four Queens represents to you the ideal mother? Of the sixteen Courts, which one carries the best archetypal energy to urgently deploy in your life right now? Would you ever trust the advice of the Page of Cups? Do you tend to organize your life's decisions according to expected patterns of behavior determined by social or any other kind of hierarchy? Which court card energy could you use better at work if you needed to confront your boss or supervisor with a serious or delicate matter?

Interpretation of cards comes down to context, correspondences, impressions, intuition, and keeping personal projections and expectations at bay. The energies of the cards say it all: the images connect to each other in magical, uncanny ways, if we just get out of the way. The more you work with a deck, the more accessible the images become and the closer the relationship you establish with them. How much material you need to study and learn before daring to read cards is rather subjective and depends on each individual's comfort zone. Some people might be more intuitive than others. But that does not translate into accuracy. Intuition is a Grace as well as a learned skill that needs to be honed, and never taken for granted because it is not ours to keep or flaunt. Ignorance is dangerous and sometimes a little knowledge when accessing the astral world of the Invisibles might serve to inflate the ego with falsity and deception.

Tarot works best when we use it as a mystical tool. The intention of both reader and querent must be clear and serving, always, the higher good. How we access the cards, how we pose the questions, how we invoke guidance along the way; everything should be practiced within a sacred field of Grace.

The Court Cards

Yet, we must be realistic and keep in mind that consulting the cards is often prompted by immediate needs and challenges that require practical answers to help us gain a better understanding of a situation. Remain open to the innumerable interpretations that Courts might have in a spread. Do not just assume that they signify people, and open your mind to whatever speaks to you directly through all your senses.

It is useful to study Tarot using a deck that follows some kind of logic, hierarchy, or cosmology. Quite often, it might be difficult to find a "logical" connection between the Courts and the rest of the Minor Arcana. They could, indeed, be two completely separate worlds, but this might not be bad at all. Find a deck that appeals to you. Use the interpretation of more traditional decks to gain valuable intellectual discipline. The decks that provide the *seed* for the present day proliferation of Tarot decks are few, and I call them "classic" for this reason. These decks were created within specific guidelines and under social, cultural and religious circumstances that were part of the collective consciousness (and subconsciousness) of that time. And the people who used them amplified and modified the meanings of the cards through the centuries. We do gain access to a wisdom that is older than we can fathom.

We cannot expect clients to be always receptive to spiritual or esoteric interpretations. It is essential, however, to deliver a balanced and congruent reading that will bring to the consciousness of the querent the needs of soul; otherwise we are failing, if not the querent, ourselves. Divination is not for everyone. Fortunetelling is something else. I believe that using Tarot as a divination and transformational tool requires that we help the clients integrate the messages received at a practical level of awareness that makes sense to them, and also at a level that touches something much deeper in themselves. We cannot ignore the spiritual dimension because we must honor message and messengers, and give thanks for the wisdom received at the end of each reading.

STUDIES ON MYSTICAL TAROT

Some Final Observations

This book presents an esoteric interpretation of Tarot Courts according to Rosicrucian tradition. We will refer mainly to the Waite-Smith deck, and to a personal color version from Builders of the Adytum. Astrological and Cabalistic connections are mentioned along the way. Please refer to the diagrams and charts provided to understand some of the connections made in this workbook. I had to wrestle with how much material to include in this brief mystical study of sixteen cards, and at what level to present it. Transformational work that uses Tarot as a tool for self-analysis and self-realization inevitably needs to address Soul and ways to gain access to higher levels of awareness.

It has been my intention to present here esoteric and Qabalistic relationships that connect mostly to the Rosicrucian and the Golden Dawn traditions, including BOTA. Not all modern decks carry an esoteric or spiritual dimension. The Rosicrucian tradition produced some of the most enduring and deepest interpretations of humanity's search for self-realization and union with the One. And I hope that some of this occult tradition is reflected in this study with sufficient clarity to help the serious student.

We will, therefore, divide the Courts according to the Holy name *Yod Heh Vav Heh* and their placement on the Tree of Life.

Let us summarize the basics: The Kings are in charge of the mandate of the kingdom. They rule the Element of Fire within their suit and they project a structure to their kingdom based on how they manage the balance of energy between Fire and their assigned World. Their domain defines their ruleship ability. How the images appear to you able to dispense or withdraw power should be carefully noted in a reading. The Kings might seem less enduring or stable than their Queen, but pay attention to other cards in a divination spread, like the Emperor or the Devil or the Magician, because there is a strong connection between the Majors and the Courts. Key IX, the Hermit, is assigned to the Hebrew letter Yod in the Golden Dawn and BOTA traditions. All the Kings reflect qualities of Yod. If you have a reading where the Hermit and a King are present, you must pay attention to the way both cards might suggest answers or potentialities to the given question.

22

The Court Cards

The Queens bring forth and realize the creative energy of the element of Water; they activate or give birth to the full potentiality of their Suit. They set in motion, nourish and develop the innate power brought forth by the King. Queens also rule the deep waters of the unconscious (the *subconscious energies of creation*) and have access to our dream body and our mental body. The power of the Queens might appear more subtle, and yet more penetrating, stabilizing and enduring than their King.

It is important to note that the letter Heh is assigned to Key IV, the Emperor, the Path of the Constituting Intelligence on the Tree of Life. The Emperor is also Ab, the Father and "the Ancient of Days." All these qualities show the integrating essence of the four Queens, who are able to exert and nourish authority because they carry the energies of the Mother and the Father. The Empress and the Emperor are here united in full glory.

The Knights carry the mandate of the kingdom and might serve their Queen more readily or willingly than their King. In the Golden Dawn, these are the Princes, the mighty sons of the King (or Knight) and Queen, but still dependent upon the activation of their power from both father and mother. The movement of the Knights in a spread often serves to indicate how other cards relate or not to their actions or reactions. Knights carry a vital force that imparts an aspect of Spirit to any reading. Carefully note how their energy impresses any specific card in a spread.

The Knights sit in Tiphareth, the Sphere of the Sun and of the Higher Self; their mystical dimensions overflow into six Sephiroth: Chesed and Geburah above, to form the *Egoic Triad*; and Netzach, Hod and Yesod below, called the *Personality Triad,* which is really a quaternity because Tiphareth is their main influence. All the Knights represent an aspect of the human spirit as Ruach, the Breath of God, and suggest ways that vibrations from Vau may radiate from the six dimensions of Yetzirah. Ruach *in-forms* the Nephesh ("soul") of the universe. This is the inspiriting or animating vital force of creation.

Pages or Knaves show an inquisitive approach to the use of the Element. This is a younger, more innocent or raw energy, perhaps an Initiate of the mysteries. Yet they respond to the accumulated energies of the three Worlds above them, and serve as "thrones" to the Aces of their suit.

23

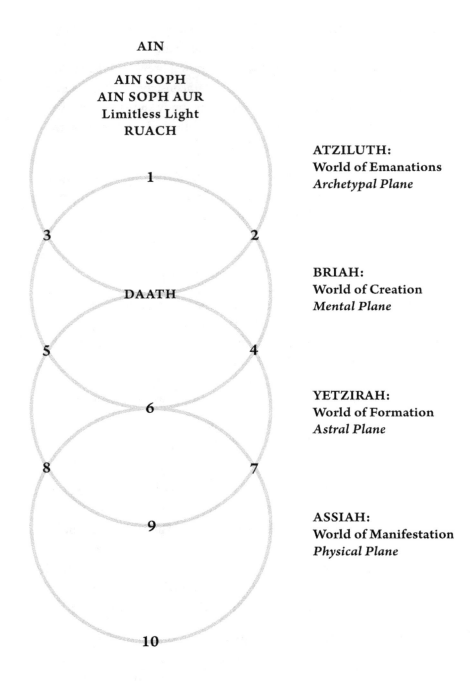

The Four Qabalistic Worlds as Concentric Circles on the Tree of Life

The Court Cards

Summary of Correspondences:

Hebrew Letter	Qabalistic World	Tarot Suit	Element	Zodiac cardinal, fixed, mutable
YOD	Atziluth Emanations	Wands	Fire	Aries, Leo, Sagittarius
Initial HEH	Briah Creation	Cups	Water	Cancer, Scorpio, Pisces
VAU	Yetzirah Formation	Swords	Air	Libra, Aquarius, Gemini
Final HEH	Assiah Manifestation	Pentacles	Earth	Capricorn, Taurus, Virgo

In the Golden Dawn the Pages become the four Princesses and are depicted as powerful Amazons that carry the Force of the Final Heh, combined with the potency of King, Queen, and Prince. They are meant to exude a mighty power, representing the solidification and materialization of the Element they embody.

I find it helpful to consider both the Knights and the Pages as forces from the archetypal, mental, astral and physical planes that respond to the energy dispensed by the Element that they serve. Keep in mind that Vau, as nail and hook, establishes relationships between the various planes of beingness and between high and lower levels of awareness. Ruach as Breath of God is everywhere, and so is Soul, no matter what name we give it. Shekhinah as the Divine Mother is also immanent and able to dwell at any level she so desires. Yet she chooses to dwell in the Final Heh: in Malkuth the densest and grossest Kingdom, to inspire us to do our Work and thus gain access to our own innate divinity.

STUDIES ON MYSTICAL TAROT

As we enter the world of the Courts, I will be referring to astrological correspondences along the way, keeping in mind that some of these correspondences are not shared by all the mystery schools associated with the Rosicrucian tradition. For example, Builders of the Adytum assigns the Ace and Page of Wands to the first Celestial Quadrant on the Zodiac Wheel corresponding to Aries, Taurus and Gemini; the second Quadrant of Cancer, Leo and Virgo is assigned to the Ace and Page of Cups; the third Quadrant (Libra, Scorpio and Sagittarius) is assigned to the Ace and Page of Swords; and the fourth Quadrant (Capricorn, Aquarius and Pisces) is assigned to the Ace and Page of Pentacles. In this arrangement the cardinal sign in the Celestial Quadrant determines the placement of Ace and Page. For other schools like the Golden Dawn, the *fixed* Zodiac sign is the determiner for the placement of Aces and Pages on the Zodiac Wheel.

The numbers from two to ten do align the same, but we will also find differences when placing the rest of the Courts according to decanates and the influence of Cardinal vs. Fixed Zodiac signs. If you work closely with astrology these inconsistencies might be annoying. Choose the placement on the Zodiac Wheel that you feel more comfortable with. At some point in our studies we most become independent from strictures that block our understanding of higher learning or that block our communication with our Inner Teacher. Spirit talks to each of us differently; we must find the right language and symbols that help us understand intuitively our personal communication with the astral world.

After a while you will realize that the Zodiac qualities are present in all of us, and that it is all a matter of degree and personal adaptation to how the planets and the Zodiac signs influence our personality vehicle. Always allow the cards and their symbols to lead the way for interpretation. In some esoteric decks the Zodiac sign and the ruling Planet are pictured on the card, already alluding to the emblematic message as envisioned by the artist. Use the emblematic message to open the channel of communication with your Inner Teacher, and then take it farther.

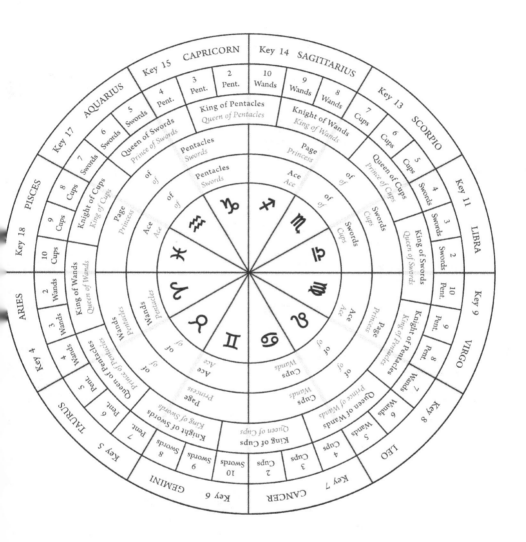

**Zodiac Wheel with Corresponding Court Decanates
According to BOTA and Golden Dawn**

27

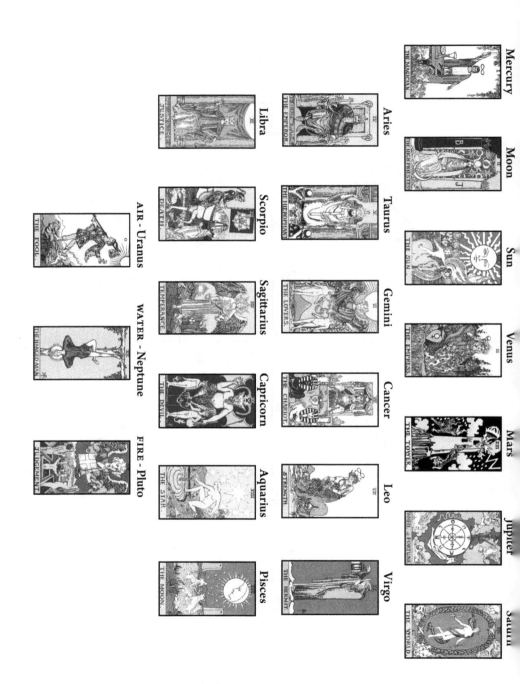

Major Arcana Planetary and Zodiac Assignments

FIRE OF FIRE	Fire of Water	Fire of Air	Fire of Earth
KING of WANDS	KING of CUPS	KING of SWORDS	KING of PENTACLES
Water of Fire	*WATER OF WATER*	Water of Air	Water of Earth
QUEEN of WANDS	QUEEN of CUPS	QUEEN of SWORDS	QUEEN of PENTACLES
Air of Fire	Air of Water	*AIR OF AIR*	Air of Earth
KNIGHT of WANDS	KNIGHT of CUPS	KNIGHT of SWORDS	KNIGHT of PENTACLES
Earth of Fire	Earth of Water	Earth of Air	*EARTH OF EARTH*
PAGE of WANDS	PAGE of CUPS	PAGE of SWORDS	PAGE of PENTACLES

Qabalistic Arrangement of the Courts

YOD

FIRE OF *FIRE*

Fire of Water

Fire of Earth

Fire of Air

The Power of YOD in Atziluth
Ab the Father in Atziluth
King of Wands - Fire of Fire
Atziluth World of Ideas; Divine World of Emanations

Lord of Flame and Lightning; King of the Spirits of Fire
ZODIAC WHEEL:
  GD: last decan of Scorpio through second decan of Sagittarius
  BOTA: last decan of Pisces through second decan of Aries

Atziluth is the archetypal world of emanations. This world must be ruled by a king who shows confidence, wisdom and intuition. The King of Wands is Fire of Fire and King of the Salamanders, as we can see in the Waite - Smith version here. He combines the qualities of Aries, Leo and Sagittarius—the three Fire signs. He represents the *Primordial Fire* of creation, also symbolized by the salamanders and the lions in the picture.

Let us start with the esoteric meanings of this card. The King of Wands is the bridge between the Majors and the Minors. His position in the deck is after Key XXI, the Universe (Golden Dawn) or The World (Waite and BOTA). He introduces the cosmology of the Lesser Arcana. As we descend into the Minors the King of Wands is supposed to lead the way. He is at the Gate, impatiently waiting for us. He personifies all the potencies of the letter Yod and represents the archetypal principle of all the masculine and feminine energies of creation. He is Ab, the Father, drawing his energy directly from Kether, the Crown. Ab is considered the Wisdom and Force behind all manifestation. The energy of Ab descends into the third Sephirah, Binah, where Aima the fertile Mother awaits impregnation. These two Sephiroth are constantly influencing each other through the power of Kether, seat of the Indivisible Self.

STUDIES ON MYSTICAL TAROT

The King of Wands is an excellent example of the complexities involved when interpreting the cards in Hermetic decks. He sits sideways, sort of, as if impatiently waiting for something. Is he being restless or vigilant? BOTA teachings note that this King represents the Sulphur of the Sages, which relates to the active principle of self-awareness; their King faces us with a soft smile of self-assurance. He is conscious of the power he exerts; he sits and draws his energy from above and guards it with confidence.

Because Kundalini energy is associated with the Wands and Yod, and also with the sex drive, we sense at some level a friction between the use of this energy to satisfy our senses or to nourish our spiritual nature. Every time we see a figure seated sideways in the Waite-Smith deck, we know that there is a mystery concealed that needs to be understood at a higher level of awareness. We must remember that one of the meanings of the letter Yod is "coition."

Mystically the King of Wands has at his disposal the spiritual energy that emanates from the cosmos and that he makes available to us through the power of intention. Primal Will— expanded into the Life-Force— is also intimated in the letter Yod and in this King.

The four Kings carry the contradictions that are inherent in the qualities of the element assigned to their suit. How they manage the dominion of their kingdom and how they delegate authority becomes their basic challenge. A stable King of Wands could be a compelling magician or shaman, provided that he draws from the Yod energy that reflects the Hermit's wisdom and not from the Mars and fiery force that often characterizes Aries and Key 16, the Tower. Using the full power of intuition and seed archetypal energies for the higher good is a boon to any king's dominion. But this is the kind of power that, if left unchecked, can create more havoc than necessary.

The King of Wands might have access to the boundless wisdom emanating from the second Sephirah, but having access does not mean knowing how to use it. The symbol of the lion that decorates his throne, as well as the salamanders biting their tail, emphasize the Force and potential power allocated to this King.

The Court Cards

In divination the ardent power of intention of this King could make him (or her) be somewhat volcanic, impulsive, or mercurial; or he might have the tendency to use the magic wand or staff to bring impromptu solutions without much concern for anyone else's needs or opinions. Cruelty and insensitivity might be the result of being too impatient and thus making decisions too fast for others' liking. He might seem impatient, but it could be because he does not suffer fools easily. Yet, this King is not ruthless. He is just very quick-witted and arrogant, and he is fully aware of his charisma and attraction, especially to the opposite sex, since he rules the Kundalini center.

The King of Wands might not be the romantic type, but his sensual passion makes up for it. He is self-assured and could easily seduce you, if his intention is set on it. He is not easily intimidated and could effortlessly force you to surrender your will.

A. E. Waite says little about the King of Wands and his use of authority. Yet, he mentions twice in the divinatory meanings that he is "honest." Honesty is a quality that takes us deeper into understanding ourselves. The King also has all the necessary esoteric symbols to be a practicant of the mysteries. He carries a large flowering wand, and connects directly to the symbols of the lions and the salamanders. He also personifies Higher Will.

The King and Queen of Wands can serve as alchemical channels of personal transformation when we understand the seed of their formidable power.

Suggested Meditation

Consider the King of Wands in relation to:
> *The Hermit,* Key 9, assigned to the letter Yod, and sign of Virgo.
> *The Emperor,* Key 4, assigned to the letter Heh, Aries, and alchemical Sulphur.
> *The Tower,* Key 16, assigned to the Planet Mars.

What connections come to your mind with these four cards? What kind of a "quaternity" could you build with these four commanding energies in your life at this moment?

35

The Power of YOD in Briah
Ab the Father in Briah
The King of Cups - Fire of Water

Lord of the Waves and the Waters; King of the Hosts of the Sea; King of the Undines, Sirens and Nymphs

ZODIAC WHEEL:
    GD: last decan of Aquarius through second decan of Pisces
    BOTA: last decan of Gemini through second decan of Cancer

BOTA assigns the first and second decanates of the Cardinal sign to each King because they give impulse to each season: the King of Wands to spring; the King of Cups to summer. This King fits the type of a Pisces, however, as depicted by Waite-Smith. Notice the pendant he is wearing and his distant, dreamy gaze. The pendant also connects this card to the Hebrew letter Nun, "fish," assigned to the fixed water sign Scorpio (Key XIII, Death).

Stop for one moment and ask yourself, "How would the Primal Fire energy influence the Primal Water of Creation? What primordial, archetypal spark could the King of Cups infuse to the waters of the subconscious?" *The term "subconscious" often indicates in these traditions the Jungian "collective unconscious."* However, there are specific instances where we cannot use both terms interchangeably; especially when speaking of the triad "sub-consciousness/self-consciousness/super-consciousness."

On the mental plane, Fire of Water intimates the ability to bring forth the spark or impulse of creativity into the world of Briah. As Ab the Father he navigates the unstable and wavy surface of his domain: the world of the subconscious. He also rules the world of feelings, emotions, and dreams. Water

The Court Cards

in this realm signifies the Sea of Creation, the world of Binah the Mother. It could also imply the alchemical water, *the water that is not wet,* as well as the expansive and adaptable qualities of the root of water. Alchemy teaches us that the marriage of Fire and Water leads to a sacred marriage of opposites (*hierosgamos*) and this *coniunctio* is a special dimension reflected in the personality of this King, who needs to bring forth dominion of fire into the kingdom of water. The subconscious is capable of generating images and forms that eventually manifest without us being able to control them. Perhaps the best lesson we can learn from the King of Cups is to remain afloat, like the ship on the background, and learn to navigate the murky waters of the *unconscious* with vigilance and humility.

Notice the short scepter (symbol of sovereignty) and the large golden cup (water and emotions) that he is holding. These two symbols indicate that he might be a fair ruler, even when representing the Yod-Fire force of Water. At times, however, the scepter and the cup might be out of balance (especially in reverse position). His tendency might be to rule with the heart more than with the mind, and he might even project callousness or shallow emotions at times. But keep in mind that all Kings carry the creative force of Yod and, as such, they are capable of drawing wisdom directly from the Master Teacher, Key IX the Hermit. There is such a depth in this card that sometimes we must backtrack, take a second, and third, look at the spread; then reflect on its meaning before "leaping" into any conclusions.

How can this King activate our volition or desire as well as our imagination in the Qabalistic World of Briah, Creation? More importantly, how could he help us balance and even cleanse or purify the lower energy centers or chakras, which are easily at the mercy of Fire and its primitive, tribal, survival instincts?

This is the card of the shaman-healer, sage, teacher, guru; he is the spiritual advisor, priest or psychological counselor. I also find that men who are very creative in the arts, such as writers, poets, painters, philosophers, etc., tend to identify more often with the King of Cups than any other court card. Ruleship of the subconscious energies of creation entails great responsibility. This King navigates the astral waters and, therefore, must maintain a

STUDIES ON MYSTICAL TAROT

fine line of separation between fantasy and reality, between the visible and invisible worlds.

Vulnerability and contradictions come to the surface when we interpret this card at the literal, symbolic and spiritual levels. The King of Cups is, basically, empathic and nurturing; and because of the fluidity inherent in the element of water, he is not good with timetables and often misses a date, or might seem forgetful or frivolous. The mythical Fisher King is an archetypal image that comes to mind when we get this card in a reading. Saturn, the Moon, and Mars are three energies that also affect this King when considering his position on the Zodiac Wheel.

Waite places the King of Cups in the middle of the waves to suggest the need to master the fluctuations of the subconscious. Other decks show him with more control of his suit. There is an intimated tension in this King, as if he needed to hold on to both cup and scepter tightly, afraid to lose his emotional stability. This King might probably feel better if he were painting, writing poems, singing a love song or just day-dreaming. And because he is "fire of water" he must have an outlet, a way to connect to his creative mind and calm his fiery impulses; otherwise, his shadow aspect would take over.

When the dolphin on the background appeals strongly to you in a reading, ask yourself, "What could be lurking deep in my subconscious that needs to come up for recognition?" Dolphins are often messengers from the gods, mermaids that guide us through the deep waters of our consciousness. Even the boat in the background could be the carrier of the message here, so pay attention, because it could indicate something that you need to just let go of.

At times, the King of Cups could represent emotional imbalance, co-dependency, or even insecurity hidden behind drug or alcohol abuse; especially if in reverse position, when it often might signal being "flooded," unstable and unable to navigate life or take control of it.

The Court Cards

The Power of YOD in Yetzirah
Ab the Father in Yetzirah
King of Swords - Fire of Air

Lord of the Wind and the Breezes; Lord of the Spirits of the Air
ZODIAC WHEEL:
  GD: third decan of Taurus through second decan of Gemini
  BOTA: third decan of Virgo through second decan of Libra

The King of Swords symbolizes the Primal Will in the World of Formation of Yetzirah. This is the world that we can claim as our own, since we rule the world of Formation through the vehicle of our personality. Yetzirah gives form to our thoughts and ideas and also rules the astral plane. We must, therefore, exert careful rulership at this level. This King helps us activate or ignite the power of discernment as well as the ability to communicate clearly and effectively.

Fire and Air are masculine energies and an interesting combination: two elements that add combustion to each other (or, at least, do not easily placate each other). Still, there is an aspect of the Hebrew letter Yod that serves this King well, because of the wisdom that he is able to dispense through the mental acuity and sharp communication skills at his command. He must be steady and balanced in thought and word and deed. If Waite's King of Cups appears at times a bit unstable, his King of Swords is the opposite. He exudes fair dispensation of justice; he is the "fire" that sparks Spirit and in-forms his planes of influence accordingly.

Hermetism teaches that the universe is mental and offers us Laws that reflect how we can use Mentalism for gaining control of our lower energies, by allowing balance and integration through basic principles that shape our

STUDIES ON MYSTICAL TAROT

character and personality. This is the King in control of the astral world and we can learn much from his direct access to Higher Wisdom.

In divination the King of Swords might represent the spark of inspiration needed for a writer to create her new work, or the necessary impulse to communicate an idea with self-confidence and skillful means. In conflict resolution he might imply fair and unemotional dispensation of justice. Sometimes he might remind us of King Solomon.

His qualities as "fire of air" could be deceiving, unless the card is in reverse position, in which case it could hint at an unfair decision, or even calculative vengeance. The fire of this King could be applied quite effectively to clear the air of unnecessary stagnation or mistrust. The generative intuition of Yod and the Air element combine in this image to symbolize a forward-thinking mind.

Compare this card to Key IV, the Emperor. The King looks younger and less severe; his throne is less austere, decorated with butterflies, sylphs and crescent moons, symbols that connect him to ruleship of the astral world. He holds his sword with the right hand and displays a ring on the left middle finger that alludes to his initiation into esoteric traditions. The word "sylph" comes from Paracelsus, the great alchemist from the 16th century who greatly influenced the Rosicrucians and the Golden Dawn. In Greek language, a *sylph* is also a butterfly. The air spirits are nearby; they form the backdrop of the kingdom.

For those who use the Golden Dawn Tarot, it is interesting to see how different the kings appear in that deck, compared to this one. In the GD deck, for example, Gemini, the mutable Air sign, rules the King of Swords and reminds us more of Waite's Knight of Swords.

In a reading the King of Swords could represent a situation that requires careful or calculated consideration, or even the need to consider a matter at a higher, spiritual level. Alchemical *separatio* is often connected to the power of discernment symbolized by the sword. This King could be a judge or diplomat; a member of the military; a dictator or tyrant. He could also be a scientist or an inventor. Sometimes the card might indicate a personal

The Court Cards

tendency by the querent to be judgmental.

We all have had our share of kings of swords in our life: a parent, teacher, boss, or a disciplinary figure. Both King and Queen of Swords usually require time to get to know them or even to begin to like them. Yet, they represent the way we can tap into the astral plane, through the power of meditation, to help us bring forth the right energies that assist us in our spiritual progression. How we access the subtle energies of the astral plane, and how these energies serve us in the Yetziratic World of Formation make all the difference in the kind of thoughts we generate, in the kind of world that we are capable of creating through will, desire and intention, and how we, ultimately, in-form, condense and manifest our thoughts in the physical world of Assiah.

The Power of YOD in Assiah
Ab the Father in Assiah
King of Pentacles - Fire of Earth

King of the Spirits of the Earth; Lord of the Wide and Fertile Land
ZODIAC WHEEL:
   GD: third decan of Leo through second decan of Virgo
   BOTA: third decan of Sagittarius through second decan of Capricorn

The closer we get to Malkuth the Kingdom, the denser the energy. The physical plane represented by Assiah accumulates the emanations from the previous Sephiroth according to how we manage our relationship with our Higher Self.

The King of Pentacles represents dominion over the power of manifestation with the Primal Fire of intention. He is the harvester who can sit on his throne and enjoy the fruits of his labor. We must be careful, however, how we arrive at this particular throne because sometimes our intent and desires could become our worst enemies when brought into manifestation on the Earth plane. The card suggests ruleship of will, intention and intuition in a manner that facilitates the condensation of matter into its full potentiality. The King of Pentacles knows how to influence creation by the power of will and/or magic. This could be a blessing and a curse, and reminds us of the myth of King Midas.

The four court cards in the suit of Pentacles offer glimpses of our own power of manifestation and suggest the great responsibility that comes along with that power. This is definitely not the kind of king who is interested in love. Come to think of it, the only King in the Waite-Smith deck that might be inclined to romance is the King of Cups. I often find the King of Pentacles

The Court Cards

showing up in questions of love or marriage when there is indifference to feelings or a strong need for financial security. Still, this King also rules the physical world of the senses, as well as the *fifth essence or Quintessence,* reflected on the emblematic Pentagram he holds.

We must always remember that our domain on Earth reflects our domain in Heaven ("as above, so below"). A. E. Waite was a mystic. In contrast with other esoteric decks that use golden coins or disks, he makes the pentagram the emblem of the fourth suit and of the fourth World of Manifestation. In this way he reminds us that every step we take on earth, that whatever it is we are manifesting, must be ruled by a self-conscious awareness of our power of manifestation. This power should reflect integration and balance between the three levels of consciousness: self-consciousness, subconsciousness, and superconsciousness.

The fifth essence or Quintessence is what connects us to Cosmic Consciousness and to wholeness (individuation). Having the ability to reign in the World of Manifestation with the Fire element as our conduit implies the need to seek our inspiration from the Higher Self whenever possible, in order to bring the Kingdom of Spirit into our everyday reality.

The King of Pentacles exudes strong self-confidence and magnanimity because he is aligned with the Consciousness of the limitless Source. The card sometimes reminds me of the Ten of Pentacles and the wise old man seated at the Gate, noticed by the children and the dogs, but not the adults. There is a secret, deep wisdom about this King of Pentacles. And, as we follow the Court of Pentacles, notice how the Queen, the Knight and, finally, the Page appear to us less burdened by material possessions and more spiritual, as we begin to approach the "end" of the deck. Unlike the Four of Pentacles in the Waite - Smith deck, which is sometimes called "the card of the miser," the King of Pentacles, is not worried about losing his worldly possessions, nor does he feel insecure about his abundant gifts and riches. He already has all he needs; he probably gives more to charity than what he keeps for his own use. He displays the Taurus sign on his throne, but he could just as easily be associated with Virgo or with Capricorn, so look at the other cards in the spread for its allegorical meaning.

43

Suggested Exercise:

What makes you lose your power?

Using the Waite-Smith deck, place in front of you Key XV, the Devil. This card can be used as an example of how we lose power or dominion by allowing shadow aspects of ourselves or others to take over our life. The Devil could reveal our densest and grossest qualities. As Lucifer, however, he is the "light bringer" and can help us gain access to self-recognition.

Ask yourself, *"What disempowers me?"*

Use the Four Kings and the power of Yod to bring clarity to your intuitive reading of the Devil's answer.

HEH

WATER OF WATER

Water of Fire

Water of Earth

Water of Air

The Power of HEH in Atziluth
Aima, the fertile Supernal Mother, in Atziluth
Queen of Wands - Water of Fire

Neshamah, the Higher Soul, as the source of all higher intuitive knowledge.
Queen of the Thrones of Flames; Queen of the Salamanders
ZODIAC WHEEL:
   GD: third decan of Pisces through second decan of Aries
   BOTA: third decan of Cancer through second decan of Leo

The four Queens sit in Binah and symbolize aspects of Neshamah, the Divine Soul. The Queen of Wands represents the archetypal sea of the unconscious or the subconscious energies of creation. Both Waite and Case associate this card with the power of Leo and the Sun, and with the Power of Suggestion.

In the Qabalistic tradition the Law of Suggestion usually corresponds to Key VIII, Strength—sign of Leo. The Golden Dawn and BOTA assign to Strength the Hebrew letter Teth, which symbolizes a "coiled serpent," thus intimating the power of Kundalini that we have discussed already with the King of Wands. In contrast with her King, however, this Queen is in no hurry to dole out her power. She is firm, steady, quietly dispensing her command of the Life Force through Aima the fertile Mother. She sits at the realm of Binah, Sephirah of Understanding and placement of the Planet Saturn. She is the Gatekeeper for this Sephirah's command of creation, and she will guide us across the Abyss and into the archetypal energies of the rest of the Sephiroth that form the Tree of Life. In a sense, she is responsible for dispensing the power of Neshamah, the Divine Soul, through our individual mastery of the subconscious, which directs and controls the Serpent power of Kundalini.

Control by suggestion is what we all seek when we work with transformational tools such as Tarot. Alchemy of soul is realized through self-inquiry and self-awareness. Control of our lower energies of manifestation leads us to higher attainment and to the *Quintessence*, which is our goal as we ascend and descend the Tree of Life. Together—the Queen of Wands and Key VIII, Strength— they form a mosaic of vibrant impressions that connect us with archetypal energies of transformation and to the conscious completion of the Great Work.

This Queen can manipulate the primal energies of transformation through the alchemical Fire. She is the Witch who knows the mysteries of the "Operation of the Sun," as proclaimed by the *Emerald Tablet*, basis of the Hermetic tradition and alchemy. Being capable of using the energy of the Sun through mental imagery and control of the subconscious is, indeed, magic. This Queen can help us understand fully the extent, width and breadth, of our powers of intention and intuition. And this opens the way to higher levels of awareness, thanks to the Water element that characterizes the Initial Heh, which brings fluidity and adaptation to the primordial Fire of the Queen. Alchemy of soul requires the right amalgamation of Water with Fire.

In contrast with the Queen of Wands from the Golden Dawn who sits with a tiger, this Queen sits on a throne carved with lions (containment and manipulation of fire energy?). A black cat sits by her side, hinting at her connection to magic and to the underworld.

Her self-confidence is such, that she poses in full regal attitude, holding a large flowering wand with one hand and a large sunflower with the other. Sunflowers and lions are symbols of the Sun, and even though the King of Wands also has this power at his disposal, it is the Queen who seems to know how to use it more effectively; perhaps because she is Water of Fire and, as such, brings the necessary receptivity to make Fire more adaptable and malleable to the needs of the mental plane that follows.

The Court Cards

As already noted, both Key VIII and the Queen of Wands control the subconscious through the Power of Suggestion. An important contrast here is that Key VIII symbolizes one of the four cardinal virtues of antiquity: Strength or Fortitude. This is the virtue that today would be assigned to controlling the lower chakras and, especially, the Kundalini energy. The gracious demeanor of this maiden dressed in white and opening the mouth of a tame and willing lion reflects the grace of humility; a grace that is definitely lacking in our Queen. It is important to understand the difference between these two "feminine" forces and how they could and do influence our Power of Suggestion.

This Queen represents a powerful and seductive magician, a sorcerer in command of the lower energies in the sea of the astral world. Her open legs suggest unabashed sensuality and her ability to manipulate Kundalini energy. Like her King, she knows how to influence sexual energies for her own purpose and needs. She also draws her power directly from the Sun and represents Bast, the Egyptian cat-goddess of sensuality, daughter of the Sun god Ra and twin sister of Sekhmet, the goddess often pictured with the head of a lion.

Nevertheless, the sunflowers serve to reinforce the mystical dimension of this card and to remind us that she is a strong source of higher intuitive knowledge and symbolizes a spiritual aspect of Neshamah, the Divine Soul.

The shadow aspects of this card are poignant reminders that we are in charge of the choices we make; choices which either liberate our soul or bind us to lower instincts. The Queen of Wands offers us the light of the Sun, but also takes us into our darkness. The archetypal energies that she offers us will determine our reality, and how we create on the mental, spiritual and physical planes.

Suggested Meditations:

Use the Queen of Wands to meditate on personal issues related to lack of power, insecurities, the need to gain self-esteem; and ways to understand how you dispense and expend vital energy and personal power. All these are issues that relate to our three lower chakras. This Queen can help bring forth subtle fire energies of transformation that might lay dormant in our soul, to help free ourselves from negative propensities that control our subconscious.

The Queen of Wands works quite effectively with Key 2, the High Priestess.

I sometimes recommend meditating with the three cards below in order to assuage any intensity that might be occurring in our life at the moment:

The Court Cards

The Power of HEH in Briah
Aima, the fertile Supernal Mother, in Briah
Queen of Cups - Water of Water

Queen of the Thrones of the Waters; Queen of Undines, Sirens and Nymphs.

ZODIAC WHEEL:
   GD: third decan of Gemini through second decan of Cancer
   BOTA: third decan of Libra through second decan of Scorpio

The Queen of Cups reflects the perfection of the creative world on the mental plane, when inspired by purified desires. She also intimates full dominion of the subconscious and of the "waters" of the astral plane. She is Aima, the fertile Mother, a much stronger or stable force than the King of Cups because she is Water of Water. This "water" adapts to anything, as it represents the World of Creation.

On the mental creative plane of Briah, the fire of Atziluth that we saw in the Queen of Wands ignites purpose, direction, inspiration, imagination. Here, in the realm of Cups, the Queen reigns supreme even with less effort. Every wish and thought is a prayer, and she knows the importance of keeping perfect balance between will, desire and creation. Her throne sits on solid ground; her blue gown and cape are reflections of the Sea of Binah. Her right foot rests on a stone; the other leg is crossed behind it, as if making a V, which connects her to Venus and Aphrodite. Seated in profile, she carries her secrets of creation and guards them closely. She could be a healer or shaman who moves between the visible and invisible realms with ease: a combination of both the High Priestess and the Empress.

STUDIES ON MYSTICAL TAROT

Sometimes we cannot help but see a connection between this Queen and her Knight, as he slowly approaches the kingdom with the golden cup of love for his Queen. But we also need to wonder what is it that preoccupies her mind with such intensity.

This Queen can nurture you as well as give you a lecture on literature, Socrates, the soul or the underworld, while getting ready to go to a psychic fair or embark on a long trip, to which she forgot to invite you and still insists that you go because you would hurt her feelings if you didn't. She could be manipulative, loving and distant at the same time. She could spend all day in a museum and forget about the house, cooking, or picking you up from school. And yet, when she opens her heart, you are trapped. She is fluid, malleable and adaptable, like water that fills and adapts to any kind of vessel. A. E. Waite describes her as "beautiful, fair, dreamy." And, because she is Water of Water in the world of Briah and the Sephirah of Binah the Mother, her dreams can, definitely, come true. Many actors (male or female) identify with this Queen.

The Queen stares intensely at her large golden chalice, which looks like a samovar or an ostensorium, with two black angels sprouting from the handles. The small cross on top of the vessel suggests a sacred artifact; could be an alchemical vessel of transformation or even the Holy Grail. Like the Queen of Wands, the Queen of Cups is able to bring forth the energies of the underworld. As ruler of the element of Water she can invoke the power of alchemical *"solutio"* or "distillation" on our behalf. The black angels could serve as psychopomps, the daemons that connect us to the unconscious and to the Land of the Dead. Look at the cherubim decorating the throne: they are mermaids or undines, and there is another cherub on the side of the throne, holding a fish (symbol of creation, fertility and multiplicity; but also of spirituality if we connect it to Christ Consciousness). The more you look at the card, the more associations you will find, because this is the subconscious world of dreams and of creative imagination. She represents, after all, the Primordial Water and an aspect of Aima the fertile Mother.

The Golden Dawn version of this card shows the Queen of Cups with an ibis, the sacred bird of Thoth. A. E. Waite places an ibis in Key XVII the Star, symbol of Aquarius. Place the High Priestess, the Star and the Queen

The Court Cards

of Cups together and meditate on the energies that these three cards bring forth. Use your creative imagination and visualization.

Negative aspects: There is a strong self-reflective quality in this card that sometimes, when in reverse position, might indicate inability to focus clearly on reality or too much self-absorption. The card could signal the need to ground ourselves, to stop dreaming or fantasizing and keep both feet on the ground. I do tend to pay attention when this beautiful energy appears in reverse position because of the impact this Queen has on our ability to align our subconsciousness with higher levels of awareness.

When both King and Queen of Cups appear in a reading, note carefully their placement in the spread. They could represent how we manage our subconscious energies of creation, from fire to water: from instinct or intention into full creativity and imagination. We create on the mental plane with the subconscious energy of will and desire. The Venus force of Desire is present in both King and Queen; and so is the Mars force of Volition, since Venus and Mars complement each other. And don't forget that the Saturn force is always part of the third Sephirah, seat of the four Queens and Key III, the Empress.

Inside the creative mental plane of Briah, Aima the Mother fertilizes our imagination and provides lush ground to seed, water, and nurture to full potentiality of expression all that will be needed on the Air and Earth planes that follow.

The Power of HEH in Yetzirah
Aima, the fertile Supernal Mother, in Yetzirah
Queen of Swords - Water of Air

Queen of the Thrones of the Air
ZODIAC WHEEL:
  GD: third decan of Virgo through second decan of Libra
  BOTA: third decan of Capricorn through second decan of Aquarius

A. E. Waite suggests in the *Pictorial Key* that the Queen of Swords is not as lofty as her King, noting that she is "scarcely a symbol of power." And yet, this might be a "blind," to distract or confuse those readers who are not students of mystery traditions. Whether we emphasize the qualities of Libra or Aquarius to interpret this card when placed on the Zodiac Wheel, we recognize that Neshamah, the Divine Soul, in the Formative World of Yetzirah can fertilize through Aima our thoughts and give them any imaginable form we dare to conceive.

This Queen signifies dominion of the Formative World, and reminds us of Key XI, Justice and sign of Libra. Both cards connect to the principles of Adjustment and Equilibrium. Like Aquarius, Key XVII, the Queen also reflects the ability to connect to the astral plane and stabilize the deep waters of the subconscious through the power of meditation.

The third Air sign, Key VI, the Lovers, assigned to Gemini, is also connected to this Queen. If you look at the Tree of Life and place the Queen of Swords on the third Sephirah, Binah, you will see how this Queen connects to Geburah, Sphere of "Severity," and to Tiphareth, "Beauty." All the Queens carry qualities from Binah and Aima into the Sephiroth below, but

The Court Cards

in this case it is worth noting that Key VI, the Lovers, is placed on the 17th Path of the Disposing Intelligence that connects Binah and Tiphareth. Key VI is assigned to the Hebrew letter Zain, "sword." Key XI, Libra, is placed on the Path of the Faithful Intelligence, connecting Geburah with Tiphareth. Tiphareth and Binah are fully reflected on each other through the Path of Zain the Sword. *This reflection through the sword of discernment brings to the egoic level ruled by Tiphareth the intuitional consciousness of Neshamah, the divine Soul. Through Libra, Tiphareth receives the necessary balance to equilibrate the Egoic Triad.*

The Queen sits sideways, hinting direct access to higher knowledge. The hilt of her sword rests on the arm of the throne, close to a cherub and butterflies—her spirit guides. The string or tassel on her left wrist could be a sign of widowhood (still used in some eastern countries). Waite tells us that "her countenance is severe but chastened: it suggests a familiarity with sorrow." We must note here that the Freemasons call themselves "Sons of the Widow" as a way to honor Hiram Abiff, the main architect of Solomon's Temple.

In alchemy both the King and the Queen of Swords could represent the act of "separatio" or of "sublimatio," just like the grey throne and cape in both cards suggest the ability to connect to higher levels of consciousness.

Some people seem to react a bit apprehensive when this card appears in a reading. Maybe is the way that she holds the sword; maybe is her apparent aloofness or suggestive sadness. This Queen is often seen as merciless, calculating and stern; with no sense of humor. This could be a reflection from the inherent qualities of Geburah as sphere of Severity. In the Golden Dawn and Aleister Crowley versions of this card, the Queen carries a sword in one hand and the severed head of a man in the other.

The Queen of Swords does not suffer fools easily; she is extremely perceptive, bright and rational, with excellent communication skills. Many of the qualities we have mentioned in the King of Swords also apply to her. Because she is the Water of Air she could help add a special fluidity and flexibility to the thought processes that characterize her suit. Both the King and the Queen of Swords open the Gate to Higher Consciousness.

Notice the clouds on the background of the card, all below her throat chakra; they suggest clarity in expressing ideas, a no-nonsense approach to life and full confidence in her own ability to rule the Air element with balance and fortitude. The sole bird flying over her head, up in the clear blue sky, is another sign of Spirit and of lofty thoughts.

Suggested Exercises:

Place the three Air signs in front of you. Notice the correspondences between them. For example, the Queen of Swords and Key XVII, the Star, can teach us the right concentration to achieve higher wisdom with the power of meditation. Key VI, the Lovers, reflects the power of Mercury and the need to bring the three levels of consciousness into total harmony and balance. Key XI, Justice, helps us balance heart and mind.

What connection can you make with these three cards in the rulership of your mind at the moment? What other "air" qualities do you find in the Queen of Swords that could be applied to the way that you formulate your intentions and desires into thoughts?

The Power of HEH in Assiah
Aima, the fertile Supernal Mother, in Assiah
Queen of Pentacles - Water of Earth

Queen of the Thrones of Earth
ZODIAC WHEEL:
   GD: third decan of Sagittarius through second decan of Capricorn
   BOTA: third decan of Aries through second decan of Taurus

A.E. Waite describes the Queen of Pentacles as having "greatness of soul." She synthesizes many of the attributes of the Divine Mother and invites us to find her in Nature and all its manifestations. Can we find the Divine in all that surrounds us? Are we capable of intending, dreaming, giving form and finally manifesting a world of peace and innate fertility?

Aima the fertile Mother appears to us now holding a large golden pentacle on her lap, as if nurturing a magical child. The pentacle intimates the Quintessence, and also the Holy Grail and the Philosopher's Stone. In alchemy the quintessence is "extracted" from the four elements in the processes utilized to achieve the Philosopher's Stone. Think of the four elements as principles and the fifth essence as the sacred Pentad, the higher principle that unites all of them.

The card suggests how the energies of the first Heh connect to the basic roots of creation reflected in Assiah, the World of Manifestation. Like Key III, the Empress, this card reminds us of Pachamama, Gaia, Rhea, Demeter, and so many other goddesses we associate with the Earth Mother. Shekhinah, the feminine essence of the Divine, dwells in Malkuth. She is God's emanating presence in all things.

STUDIES ON MYSTICAL TAROT

There is a soft mystic quality to this card; we sense a sort of sacred lushness surrounding this Queen and, in case we missed the implied Hermetic symbolism, the rabbit nearby reminds us that she is also Aima the fertile mother in the physical world. The Queen represents all the potentiality of bringing the full force of creation into manifestation.

The throne is gray, decorated with the earthy symbols of gnomes, a bull and a goat. The bull alludes to the fixed Earth sign of Taurus and the goat to the cardinal Earth sign Capricorn, as well as to rituals of fertility from early traditions.

Both the Hierophant and the Devil are essential aspects of her domain. The goat is a controversial sign; in Christianity it is often associated with Paganism and the Devil. Both goat and pentagram are embraced by the Golden Dawn to signify ancient rituals of purification and fertility. The goat emblem on her throne also emphasizes the "earthy," sensual quality of her element, which she offers to us like a silent blessing. We are once again reminded that in the rites of mystery traditions, the body serves as the vessel to seek union with the One. *"Kether is in Malkuth and Malkuth is in Kether."* This is the Queen that shows us the way to spiritual perfection through the purification of our vehicle of expression, of our body: the athanor of alchemical transmutation.

Suggested Exercise:

1. Draw a five-pointed star on a piece of paper.

2. Take the four Queens, the Empress and the High Priestess and place five of them on the pentagram, leaving one of the cards aside.

3. After you have placed five of the six cards on the diagram, take the last card and set it in the center of the pentagram.

4. Now, look at the six cards and their placement inside of the pentagram and ask yourself why you placed the cards the way you did, especially the one card in the center of the pentagram.

5. How does the card in the center relate to the other five at this point in your life?

VAU

AIR OF AIR

Air of Water

Air of Fire

Air of Earth

The Power of VAU in Atziluth
Ruach as the human spirit in Atziluth
Knight of Wands - Air of Fire

GD: Prince of the Chariot of Fire
ZODIAC WHEEL:
   GD: third decan of Cancer through second decan of Leo
   BOTA: third decan of Scorpio through second decan of Sagittarius

The knight is supposed to activate and implement the mandate of the kingdom. But, he might even kill the king and marry the queen; or at least have an affair with the queen, as many myths and fairy tales tell us. There is usually a mystique surrounding the knight that often makes him a more interesting figure than the king. The Golden Dawn Magical Tarot, for example, pictures them as Princes in chariots exuding the regal energy of their suit. They represent the vehicle of the personality and the alchemical transformative power of Vau.

Understanding the knights as vehicle of the personality and aspect of the human spirit in search of wholeness or self-containment is one of the messages that the Hebrew letter Vau tries to convey. Vau can be interpreted as the conjunction "and" when placed as a prefix. Interconnection is one of the tasks of any warrior or knight, who not only fulfills the kingdom's mandate, but also maintains the energy of connectivity of the kingdom with the outside world.

The knight is the archetypal rescuer in shining armor. The Knight of Wands and his horse are energized, like all the cards in the suit of Wands, by the element of Fire and the energy of the Sun. He represents swiftness in action, the knight summoned by his king to save the kingdom. He is ignited by the

STUDIES ON MYSTICAL TAROT

fire of intention and thrives on quests. Like the charioteer in Key VII or the rider of the Six of Wands, he returns to the kingdom with gifts of power and glory. Yet, somehow, when we take a second look at the Knight of Wands, we might not be convinced that we should place our kingdom, the Queen, our savings, our 401K or, even worse, our young virginal Princess daughter in his care and custody. Air and Fire make a dangerous combination. This Knight is all fired up, seeking adventure and thrills, and he might be too unpredictable; where are horse and Knight going with all that loose energy?

A. E. Waite tells us in his *Pictorial Key* to look at the motion of the horse as an expansion of the character of its rider. We must do so with all the Knights to extract a fuller meaning from the cards' image-concepts. All the BOTA Knights, for example, ride intrepid horses as symbols of the full potentiality that Ruach as Breath of Life offers us at each level of awareness.

When you get the Knight of Wands in a reading it might signal time for reflection, or the need to make sure that you are not being too impetuous arriving at a decision or energizing new ventures without careful consideration. But there might be other times when this card might indicate the right archetypal energy necessary to perform a task, launch a venture, or quickly resolve a situation, leaving heart and mind behind.

Qabalistically, the Knights sit in Tiphareth, the seat of the Ego and center from which energies of transformation are filtered and communicated to the domains above and below. They represent active energies ready to bring forth the needed qualities for our spiritual progression. Tiphareth is the Gate to the Egoic Triad as well as to the Personality Triad; it helps us unite with Soul and with our own divinity. This is why it is also called the seat of the Christ Consciousness.

When Vau connects us with the intuitive power of the Hierophant as the Inner Voice of Intuition, and as an igniting force of will, ideas and imagination in Tiphareth, we are presented with an opportunity for self-transformation that can take us to new dimensions in our spiritual progression.

Ruach at this level or plane represents the human spirit, centered in Tiphareth. Ruach is pure consciousness, and it takes form through the

The Court Cards

power of vibration. The challenge of the four Knights is to reach the necessary level of awareness or the vibratory level that would assure their actions to be in harmony with the Higher Self. From Tiphareth, the Knights move into the upper Sephiroth of Memory and Volition igniting vital energies of transformation. Below Tiphareth we find the Sephiroth of Desire, Intellect and the astral consciousness that sits in Yesod in urgent need to connect to higher vibratory levels for purification and transformation.

Notice how both the Knight of Wands and the Knight of Swords in the Waite-Smith deck are fully engaged in action. At a mystical level, both cards can be employed to stir our spirit and help us destroy falsity as we search union with the One. Perceived this way, the Knight of Wands is offering himself fully to our creative imagination and to our World of Formation. The Ego that sits in Tiphareth uses the four Knights to activate the human spirit as it moves through the four worlds and the various Sephiroth of personality and thus helps us reach our full potentiality.

The Power of VAU in Briah
Ruach as the human spirit in Briah
Knight of Cups - Air of Water

GD: Prince of the Chariot of the Waters
ZODIAC WHEEL:
  GD: third decan of Libra through second decan of Scorpio
  BOTA: third decan of Aquarius through second decan of Pisces

All the Knights have the ability to carry and anchor the power of the Suit and Element that they represent. With the King of Cups in the middle of the wavy sea, the Knight of Cups is now in charge of carrying the King's mandate on land. But, take a look at his demeanor and at the horse he rides. They don't seem to be in any hurry. No wonder the Queen of Cups needs to be attentive while seated on rocky, but still solid ground. Place the three cards next to each other in front of you. How do the energies flow from one card to the other? Try to imagine how the Knight of Cups could fulfill the mandate of the Briahtic kingdom.

Versions of the Grail legend are present in Waite's Minor Arcana, and this is the Knight who is more in love with romance than with adventure. Does he represent Lancelot or Percival? In the earlier versions of the Grail myth, Percival brings to the Queen and the kingdom the fertility lacking in the barren Fisher King. Is that what his cup intimates? The Knight and his horse connect us to Key XIII, Death, assigned to the Hebrew letter Nun, "fish", and to the fixed Water sign Scorpio, another symbol of fertility. The resemblance between this card and Key XIII could be interpreted as the symbolic death in alchemy of the King and the birth of a new King. In addition, the Knight's horse is gray, which signals union of opposites and serves as symbol of spiritual growth and maturity.

The Court Cards

Air of Water alludes to a combination of mind, thoughts, heart and emotions. This is useful in certain situations that demand a deep descent into subconscious energies like in soul retrieval or dream visualization. The qualities reflected by this Knight are welcome in careers that require cautious thinking and a caring disposition, like the medical profession. The winged helmet and the spurs reinforce the intellectual quality of Air, also assigned to Mercury - Hermes. Note the red fish (Scorpio and Mars) and the undulating water symbols on his garment. Aquarius and Pisces come here to mind; which are, incidentally, the two Zodiac signs that BOTA assigns to this card. There might be self-absorption in this Knight, as well as dreaminess and romanticism, like someone who is in love with love. Sometimes his pose could refer to careful and intentional seduction rather than romance. Nevertheless, this card is a carrier of human spirit into higher dimensions. A. E. Waite reminds us that the card can sometimes refer to "higher graces of the imagination."

Perhaps the Knight of Wands prepared the way for the Knight of Cups to focus on transferring energies of transformation from one plane to the other. Creativity in the mental plane needs to be infused with the right sparks of intention and intuition; they need to percolate through all the spheres of influence that affect the human personality. The Knight of Cups must work with the waters of the unconscious with care. Vau in the mental-desire plane of Briah is all about creativity and connectivity. This Knight represents intuitional knowledge acquired through intense work at all the levels of Ruach.

It is up to us to bring forth the necessary strength and fortitude to access and gain dominion over the Briahtic waters of creation. This is the Knight who studies, meditates, enters the murky waters of the astral world trying to penetrate the mystery of the cosmic forces of creation. The message that the Golden Dawn Prince of the Chariot of the Waters reveals to us is very similar to Waite's and BOTA's.

Going back to divination mode, the "shadow" aspects of this card might include unnecessary postponement in accomplishing a task; or inability to make a firm commitment, especially in matters of romance. Sometimes the card can signal treason or betrayal; or it might hint at something mysterious or hidden, such as ulterior motives or conniving intentions.

Suggested Exercise:

Balancing the Chakras: The Knight of Cups gives us an intimation of the unfoldment of the human spirit in the creative plane. This card lends itself to a deeper understanding of ourselves as vehicles of expression for the Primal Will or Indivisible Self reflected in Kether. Death and rebirth as a journey through the various levels and spheres of consciousness is intimated with this card.

Place in front of you the Major Arcana cards for Cancer, Scorpio, Pisces and Aquarius. Qabalistically, Key VII the Chariot also represents the vehicle of personality. Visualize how the Page of Cups moves back and forth through all these cards. Pay close attention to how this movement affects your energy centers: do you feel one card strongly in one chakra over another? What kind of emotions or thoughts arise when you connect with these cards at a subconscious level?

Use Arcanum XVII to balance the energy centers and "fix" any volatile quality that impresses you.

Cancer	Scorpio	Pisces	Aquarius

The Court Cards

The Power of VAU in Yetzirah
Ruach as the human spirit in Yetzirah
Knight of Swords - Air of Air

GD: Prince of the Chariot of the Wind
ZODIAC WHEEL:
   GD: third decan of Capricorn through second decan of Aquarius
   BOTA: third decan of Taurus through second decan of Gemini

From the archetypal world of will and ideas to the creative world of mind activated by desire, we now get closer to that level of the astral plane where the full consciousness of the human spirit gives shape and form to every thought we generate. The Knight of Swords is Air of Air. He represents the forces of the personality complex on the astral plane. He is capable of mediating between above and below through the agency of Tiphareth and the innate power of Vau.

The card at first glance might imply volatility, a hasty action, a person who launches forward aimlessly, carried by airy thoughts and without considering or pondering the consequences. It reminds us of Don Quixote de la Mancha. A. E. Waite in the *Pictorial Key* compared him to Sir Galahad, describing him as "clean of heart."

Chivalry, skill and bravery are part of the message of the card; if we are in a dire situation, this might be the knight to call to our rescue. But, we need to be careful how we utilize this kind of impulsive and aggressive behavior before we activate the card's potentiality. Contrast the horse in this card with the Knight of Wands, for example. Wands represent the impulse, the intent that sparks action; Swords often indicate result, or reaction; the way that our impulses, will, and desire form our thoughts and manifest in our

STUDIES ON MYSTICAL TAROT

daily life. Here we find horse and horseman suspended in mid-air, completely immersed in their domain. His saddle is decorated with butterflies, an alchemical symbol of spirit, but also associated with something ephemeral and impermanent. The red birds could intimate passion in flight. If this Knight appears in a reading to be flying on your behalf, catch him and use him accordingly. This might be the kind of energy that you need to hone in yourself. He can also assist in dispersing any energy stagnation and might lend his sword to help you "separate the subtle from the gross," to quote the *Emerald Tablet*, to make your soul journey lighter and less toxic.

Sometimes we need a knight that can move back and forth between the worlds with ideas that lead to the right manifestation. This is, indeed, the characterization of a quick, witty and swift intellect; these are also the whirlwinds of our mind and if we learn to tame them, we might then be able to reach higher levels of spiritual awareness.

The Knight of Swords might appear in a reading to suggest the need to quiet the mind; to choose our battles more carefully; to make sure that the energy being spent is worth the effort in a given cause or problem. This might be a card of action but, unless we understand its power, we might not know which side of his double-edge sword we should use.

Waite's Knight reminds us of the King of Swords in the Golden Dawn deck. Sometimes he is also equated with the "Angel of Death." Yet, Waite wanted his Knight to represent the pure energy of the intellect unchained. Today, however, we tend to interpret this figure as a restless, fearless, or even reckless mind. Interesting enough, these were the qualities that in earlier times were attributed to the card in reverse.

Consider the mystical dimensions of the Knight of Swords: How do you envision the spiritual mandate of this Knight as active agent in your own progression? What aspect of this Knight resonates with the Vau energy connecting to Key V, the Hierophant?

The Knight of Swords prepares the way for the Knight of Pentacles in the World of Assiah.

The Power of VAU in Assiah
Ruach as the human spirit in Assiah
Knight of Pentacles - Air of Earth

GD: Prince of the Chariot of Earth
ZODIAC WHEEL:
   GD: third decan of Aries through second decan of Taurus.
   BOTA: third decan of Leo through second decan of Virgo.

The Ego in Tiphareth regulates our level of awareness. The five senses concentrate differently in each Sephirah, as well as filter through Tiphareth. How we align with our Higher Self and with our Inner Teacher can make all the difference as we assess our journey and our goals. What are we to do when we observe ourselves from the level of Assiah and realize how our actions have formed the reality that we live each day? How do we retrace our steps and become more conscious on our journey to self-realization?

Vau infuses our consciousness; we must be aware of how this infusion permeates our breath and soul, and how we respond to the Inner Voice that helps us understand the significant role each of us must play in the cosmos, including the way we relate to Mother Nature.

This card might feel a bit static, or even heavy at first sight. Yet, the Knight of Pentacles carries the Vau - Air energy of the Tetragrammaton into the Assiah of Malkuth, the Kingdom on Earth. The feminine attributes of both Cups and Pentacles make both of Waite's Knights receptive to the energies from above. Receptivity requires quietude of spirit and vigilance, to be able to understand the forces of the astral world.

STUDIES ON MYSTICAL TAROT

Both Knights in Briah and Assiah process the impulses from the worlds that precede them with careful demeanor, mindful of the impact these energies will have in their own world. Think of the four Knights as spiritual warriors, each dependent upon the other for higher awareness in order to align subconsciousness, self-consciousness and superconsciousness.

The Knight of Pentacles represents duty and responsibility. His dark horse, feeling the heaviness of their obligation, adds a saturnine quality to the picture. Air as Ruach is the Breath of God, the breath of creation. In contrast with BOTA, here knight and horse are firmly grounded, just like the Golden Dawn Prince of Pentacles, who appears heavy, pensive and stubborn like the bull slowly pulling his chariot. Both Knight and Prince of Pentacles carry the mandate of the King and Queen into the World of Manifestation and into the density of Mother Earth.

Sometimes this card appears to indicate a task that carries heavy responsibility; or it might signal the need to be fully conscious and mindful of the peaks and vales of our journey. There is a quiet sense of resoluteness in this Knight; perhaps even of unshakeable faith as he holds the Pentacle that connects us to Soul and the Quintessence. While the Queen contemplates her pentacle and "may see worlds therein," (see *Pictorial Key*), this Knight holds the symbol as a precious trophy for the world to see. Perhaps he is holding the Holy Grail or even the Philosopher's Stone.

The Great Work of humanity must be carried out in the world of Yetzirah. This is the world that allows us to gain access to our Higher Self and that connects us with all the necessary tools for our spiritual and physical transmutation.

At some point in our studies we need to ask: In what ways am I giving form (*in-forming*) to the reality that I experience every day? The Christ Consciousness that sits in Tiphareth is the Buddha Consciousness, the awakened consciousness. Awareness of our Self fulfills our mandate to *Know Thyself*. We have the power to instigate, inspire, create and manifest reality. We must move from ego to the One Ego in Tiphareth, no matter how many lifetimes it will take. This is our mandate.

The Court Cards

Suggested Exercise

1. Now that you have had a chance to review the Knights as reflections of Vau and of our personality vehicle, place all four in front of you and ask yourself, which aspect of the Higher Self needs to be stirred within you. Draw one card from the rest of your Tarot deck and see how this card is reflected in each of the Knights. Don't forget to write your impressions on your journal.

2. Use the three Earth signs as Gates to understand how the Knight of Pentacles could serve in connecting us to the physical plane of Assiah. Write down your impressions on your journal as you move from one card to the other asking pertinent questions about your personal journey.

FINAL HEH

EARTH OF EARTH

Earth of Fire

Earth of Water

Earth of Air

The Court Cards

The Power of the Final HEH in Atziluth
Page of Wands - Earth of Fire
Throne of the Ace of Wands

GD: Princess of the Shining Flame and the Rose of the Palace of Fire
ZODIAC WHEEL:
   GD: Quadrant of Cancer/Leo/Virgo.
   BOTA: Quadrant of Aries/Taurus/Gemini

The Pages or Knaves are often considered young valets, messengers or foot soldiers whose role is to run errands and bring primal energies to a given situation. They are meant to show inquisitiveness about the use of their element as *condensed or materialized energy*. In other words, since they represent Earth, they are responsible for the final condensation, coagulation and transformation of the energy that their suit represents.

Pages correspond to the final Heh of the Tetragrammaton, and they are interpreted as a feminine or receptive energy. Again, this classification has nothing to do with

the sex of the individual or the situation being addressed, but rather with the *quality of receptivity*. Their seat in Malkuth reminds us of their connection to Shekhinah and Kallah the Bride, thus making a spiritual link with the Knights seated in Tiphareth.

The fact that Pages or Princesses are placed on the Zodiac Wheel in the same physical quadrant with their Aces, already intimates a much higher symbology than mere messengers or foot soldiers. We need to understand that the potentiality of manifesting the forces offered to us by the Aces seated in Kether the Crown will depend on our individual spiritual unfoldment

77

STUDIES ON MYSTICAL TAROT

and on how we reflect the Tree of Life in our personality, which is our vehicle of expression of the Divine Light.

In alchemy, for example, the Pages could reflect aspects of the so-called "fixing of the volatile," which alludes to their ability to hold and ground the volatile quality of their element in order to produce the Philosopher's Stone.

In the world of archetypes, the Page of Wands brings forth the physical and concrete manifestation of her element through the careful manipulation of the fire of intention and her sharp intuition. As the "throne" of the Ace of Wands, her responsibility is to safeguard and make available to us the Kingdom of Malkuth as we embark on a new project, or as we seek higher understanding in any situation; or perhaps as we ground our intuition and project it into the creative world. This Page embodies quiet impeccability, thoughtful and intentional action. Notice his regal garment. There is a strong relationship between the Page of Wands and Key 0 the Fool in this tradition. The rich garment that Waite's Fool wears shows the emblem of the Hebrew letter Shin, the Mother Letter assigned to Fire.

As the final Heh the Pages are connectors between the various worlds as well as containers of the root of the element. The youth and demeanor of the Pages, inquisitively holding the emblem of their suit, suggest that they are Initiates of the Hermetic traditions. The seriousness of their task requires responsibility, careful consideration, and studious application. If you were given the responsibility of manifesting on Earth with the Primal Fire of Intention, how would you go about it? What qualities could your fiery energy bring to the world of manifestation? More importantly, if this power were granted to us, how would we apply it for the higher good? We all carry the archetypal First Whirling of the universe. There is a spark of Kether the Crown in all of us.

How do you see yourself concretizing and bringing forth the potentiality of the Ace of Wands through the Page of Wands? What would happen if you combine the potentiality of power offered by the Ace of any suit with the grounding and solidifying energy of any Page?

The Court Cards

Suggested Exercise:

Combine the Aces with the Pages of the other suits. You will find that the fusion of these two cards, even if from different elements, might be quite useful to concretize the ability of the Pages with the potentiality offered by the Aces.

Ponder these two examples:

The Power of the Final HEH in Briah
Page of Cups - Earth of Water
Throne of the Ace of Cups

GD: Princess of the Waters; Lotus of the Palace of the Floods
ZODIAC WHEEL:
  GD: Quadrant of Libra/Scorpio/Sagittarius
  BOTA: Quadrant of Cancer/Leo/Virgo

A. E. Waite notes that this Page is "somewhat effeminate" and "contemplating the pictures of the mind taking form." Both Earth and Water are "feminine" elements, and this Page is intentionally androgynous, although other versions show her as Princess of Cups. Look at the way she is dressed: pink tights and shirt. Her aqua dress and hat remind us of the pond in the Ace of Cups. Remember that there is a strong Qabalistic connection between the Aces and the Pages in this tradition. The Page smiles softly to the fish coming out of her cup.

The Golden Dawn Magical Tarot gives us a Princess in the middle of the sea holding a turtle coming out of a cup in one hand and a lotus flower in the other. She is wearing emblems of swans in her crown, her belly, and her legs, three key chakras or energy centers: a strong symbol of graceful creative power. She is Earth of Water as well as Princess and *Empress* of Nymphs and Undines. In fact, all the Princesses in the Golden Dawn deck are Amazon figures projecting the strength of manifestation of the Element that they represent through the vibrations of the final Heh.

The Page of Cups encapsulates the power of uniting, "linking," like the Hebrew letter Heh signifies, the world of archetypes or emanations with the

The Court Cards

world of creativity. The act of solidifying mental concepts and images allows us to co-create our reality. She needs to catch and solidify the archetypal energies from the collective unconscious and prepare them for the next plane. Imagination and creativity are the two key faculties offered to us by this Page. However, what to do with the fish coming out of our cup? Contrast the dolphin from the King of Cups with the fish from the cup that this Page is holding. A dolphin coming out of the deep sea does not surprise us, while a fish in a golden cup might. It just depends on how we condense and manifest creative ideas. A fish is a rather complex symbol; it could relate to prolific creativity, to illusion and fantasy, or to Christ Consciousness and spirituality.

The Page of Cups, representing our mental body, carries strong implications about the way that we approach the Source of our creative mind. It also represents our emotional vehicle of expression as the combined forces of Malkuth, Kallah the Bride, and the Final Heh. Binah the Mother is always present in these energies, and we cannot help but see a strong connection between the Page of Cups and the Queen of Cups, who personifies the depth of the creative waters of the unconscious.

This Page invites us to be curious about things that are not even logical, to activate imagination and visualization, and to dream; but also to contain our fantasies within parameters that keep us grounded and able to use effectively the energies of manifestation. The fish could symbolize a daemon or spirit guide. In divination sometimes the Page of Cups could mean a message being delivered from our dream body, or astral body. If you are expecting a marriage proposal, however, I would be cautious.

The card might indicate the need to meditate or go within to hear the Inner Voice that guides us. Pay attention when the Page and the Ace of Cups are present in a spread. Because this Page is the "earth of water," it might imply strong ability to concretize and give material form to ideas, wishes, and dreams. This could be either positive or negative, depending on how the subconscious tends to manifest itself in your everyday reality. Remember that pages and knaves often signal a young or immature energy.

The power of synthesizing the world of Briah in Malkuth requires strong receptivity and inquisitiveness. In Qabalah the World of Creation comes

STUDIES ON MYSTICAL TAROT

before the World of Formation. Every wish and spark of yearning acquires on the mental plane the potential to manifest, because they combine the forces of Mars and Venus, volition and desire. We must be aware and mindful of what we are feeding the subconscious at all times.

Take careful note of the shadow aspects of this card because sometimes it might warn us about the ways that we gain access to the world of elementals and to the astral plane. There is a strong connection between Malkuth and the ninth Sephirah, Yesod, Sphere of the Moon and portal to the astral plane. This is where the forces below our subconscious awareness reside, and where we need to start our ascent on the Tree of Life and gain a better understanding of ourselves.

Suggested Exercise:

Alchemical transformation by using the "alchemical water" as principle of change, growth and purification could be used quite effectively with the Page of Cups. As we tap the deep waters of the unconscious and ask our Guides and Teachers to help us align with the Superconscious energies of the Higher Mind, use the Ace and Page of Cups to bring balance to the way that you connect between the mental and the astral planes.

The Court Cards

The Power of the Final HEH in Yetzirah
Page of Swords - Earth of Air
Throne of the Ace of Swords

GD: Princess of the Rushing Winds; Lotus of the Palace of Air
ZODIAC WHEEL:
   GD: Quadrant of Capricorn/Aquarius/Pisces
   BOTA: Quadrant of Libra/Scorpio/Sagittarius

The Page of Swords suggests the need to ground or stabilize the volatility of the element of Air. If we combine the Qabalistic worlds of Formation, Yetzirah, and Manifestation, Assiah, into the meaning of this card, we could interpret the Page's attitude as hesitant, even a bit nervous or insecure, thinking about the great responsibility of safeguarding the "roots of the powers of Air," as the Ace of Swords symbolizes.

The Page of Swords projects how the astral plane exercises control over our vehicle of expression, over our personality and thoughts; and now on the physical plane his duty could well be to help us continue to refine our thoughts, desires, and intentions from the previous planes through the alchemical act of "*separatio*." This is the act that "separates the subtle from the gross" and gives us the opportunity to lift mind and heart above the usual propensities that weigh us down and dulls our inner and outer Light.

A. E. Waite describes the Page as a "lithe, active figure...in the act of swift walking... passing over rugged land..." This description fits better the BOTA Page of Swords, because Waite's Page, as presented here, looks frozen in time and space, carefully holding a heavy double-edge sword with both hands, and hair flying in the wind. She cautiously looks over her shoulder,

83

STUDIES ON MYSTICAL TAROT

with a look not of fear but rather of apprehensive awareness. How do astral forces function on the physical plane and how do they affect us in our thinking? We need to be aware that we are surrounded by Invisibles and elementals and that spiritual work requires that we remember at all times that "like attracts like." We must be vigilant. Our thoughts define us; our mind must be alert and clear in order to connect to lofty thoughts and to the creative forces that help with our physical and spiritual transmutation from heavy lead into gold. Symbolically, this is also the alchemical wedding of the Sun and the Moon, as Kallah the Bride moves up the Tree of Life to meet her spouse in Tiphareth.

Ten birds fly above making the sign of a fish. The symbol brings to mind the Page of Cups, as if the fish that was coming out of the golden Cup on the mental plane has now transformed into ten birds. The magical number ten implies endings and beginnings and offers new potentialities for growth. The birds serve as spirit guides from the astral plane ready to inspire us to co-create with our thoughts. The Page of Swords can help us give form to our thoughts, activating the power of the mind on the astral plane.

The element of Air is also the element of Ruach, "the Breath of God," "the Holy Spirit." The Fool, Key 0, also connects to Ruach. The citrine color of the Page's undergarment is a symbol of spiritual quest in both BOTA and Golden Dawn. This citrine color should also be evident in the undergarment of the Fool. Both this Page and the Fool are making similar poses with their feet.

The "earth of air" grounds our thoughts and determines the form that we give to thoughts on the physical plane. We need to understand that distorted mental images lead us to suffering and this is why Swords are often considered a difficult suit.

We control the vibratory level of our astral body through the light or darkness that we allow into our life. Through breathing techniques, chanting, vibrational color techniques, and other rituals we learn to reach higher levels of awareness that assist us in our spiritual transmutation. I often see the Page of Swords as alchemical "*sublimatio*" because this is an example of how the power of Ruach on the physical plane can lift our thoughts and

The Court Cards

spirit to a higher level. The subtle and hidden powers in ourselves can be more attainable by the powers of separation and sublimation. When we can "ground" our astral body in the Kingdom of Malkuth we might feel as light as a feather, because we have liberated our mind and have connected heart and mind with the infinite Vau of Breath and Spirit. This is the realm where the Life-Breath makes itself available to us to help us perfect our body, soul and spirit and connect us to the One.

The Pages always remind us of the need to look at the essence of the element they represent in all its potentiality and carefully learn how to apply it for the higher good. If we were given the full potentiality of manifestation in the Kingdom of Earth through the power of mind and word and deed, then we might be more careful and watchful of the weapon of thought, because as the old adage warns us, *"every thought is a prayer."*

There is a strong contrast between Waite's Page of Swords and the Princess of Swords of the Golden Dawn. The dark severity of this Princess and the symbol of the Medusa she carries as her emblem hint at a stark sense of vengeance and potential for unnecessary mental cruelty. Just imagine having such a character in charge of materializing the thoughts of her Royal Court. She could even be described as the Avenging Angel of the Courts.

The Power of the Final HEH in Assiah
Page of Pentacles - Earth of Earth
Throne of the Ace of Pentacles

GD: Princess of the Echoing Hills; Rose of the Palace of Earth
ZODIAC WHEEL:
    GD: Quadrant of Aries/Taurus/Gemini
    BOTA: Quadrant of Capricorn/Aquarius/Pisces

What binds or connects us to the material world and to the world of the senses? The Page of Pentacles carefully carries the vibrations of the final Heh of the Tetragrammaton into the World of Assiah—the world of manifestation. She stands in Malkuth the Kingdom, domain of Shekhinah and Kallah the Bride. The consolidation and integration of "earthy earth" qualities in this Page or Princess adds an immediate special dimension to this card that is hard to ignore. This Page is supposed to represent the most solidified manifestation of the element of Earth and yet there is a tenderness and warm spirituality surrounding this image of youth in quietude, contemplating the Quintessence carved in the golden pentagram that she so carefully holds.

This is one of my favorite cards in Crowley's Thoth deck, as created by Ms. Frieda Harris, because she managed to capture the essence of the message of not just the Disks, and Assiah, but of the processes available to any of us when using Tarot as an alchemical tool for personal transformation. The Princess of Disks in the Thoth deck is a moving interpretation of the Earth Mother, deeper than the Queen or Page of Pentacles from any other Golden Dawn tradition deck.

The Court Cards

Every Page carries a very symbolic, mystical resonance and we need to look hard and long; take the time to ponder how the celestial or Zodiac Quadrant assigned to them influences their role as gatekeepers of Malkuth the Kingdom. BOTA assigns the Page of Pentacles to the Quadrant of the Winter Solstice that carries us into Spring, encompassing Capricorn / Aquarius / Pisces. Symbolically, this dimension represents our cycle of physical, mental and spiritual renewal, the time of our liberation from darkness into Light, of renewal and rebirth.

In divination the Page of Pentacles might indicate the need to pay attention to our spiritual development if we are overly concerned with material possessions, financial stability, sensual needs, or any other aspect of the material and physical worlds. The card may appear in a reading when the querent is about to embark on a project that might require careful consideration and self-inquiry. It might even warn us to pay attention to our steps, to how we are treading in life; to be alert and stay centered. Pages in Malkuth are close to the astral world of Yesod, and they can easily serve as messengers or foot soldiers between the physical and the astral planes.

This Page could signal a need for soul-searching and careful introspection in a reading; it could also point at something that must be taken seriously or cared for in a special manner. The ability to manifest and co-create in our Earth domain carries a big liability. Waite carefully notes that the pentacle in this picture is "hovering" over the raised hands of this young individual. Like an orb, daemon, or spirit, the pentagram is held by this Page as something sacred, which, in fact, is.

Diligence in our alignment with nature and self-inquiry about our innermost soulful needs are essential at this stage of our journey. Both the Page and the Knight of Pentacles feel the heaviness of their responsibility in their domain on Earth and their duty to avoid the bondage that often attaches itself to our senses.

Saturn is very present here: in the sign of Capricorn and in the Arcanum XXI, the World, which closes the Major Arcana and connects the astral world of the ninth Sephirah, Yesod, with the last Sephirah, Malkuth.

The Page of Pentacles closes the deck and, like the Fool, leaves us with more questions than answers. She could, however, become the Gatekeeper who leads us into a richer, more meaningful world and who teaches us how to utilize our power of manifestation in the Kingdom of Earth as it is in the Kingdom of Heaven.

Suggested Exercise:

Take a few minutes to ask yourself how you usually form your thoughts into action and how every action generates a reaction with incalculable consequences in yourself and others. Take a closer look at the Page of Wands, the Page of Cups and the Page of Swords and ask them how they could help you manifest a more balanced life that could better apply the qualities offered to us by the Page of Pentacles.

Bibliography and Suggested Reading:

Book T - The Tarot. Available for download at http://www.tarot.org.il/Library/Mathers/Book-T.html

Case, Paul Foster. *The Tarot: A Key to the Wisdom of the Ages.* Builders of the Adytum, 1990.

_____. *Hermetic Alchemy: Science and Practice.* The Golden Dawn Tarot Series 2, 2009. Publication first appeared in 1931 as part of the lessons of The School of Ageless Wisdom.

Cicero, Chic and Sandra Tabatha Cicero. *The Golden Dawn Magical Tarot.* St. Paul, MN: Llewellyn Publications, 2001.

Fortune, Dion. *The Mystical Qabalah.* York Beach, ME: Samuel Weiser, Inc. 1984. 1st edition 1935, London.

Ginsburgh, Rabbi Yitzchak. *The Hebrew Letters: Channels of Creative Consciousness.* Jerusalem: Gal Einai Publications, 1990.

Greer, Mary K. and Tom Little. *Understanding the Tarot Court.* Woodbury, MN: Llewellyn Publications, 2004.

Hauck, Dennis William. *The Emerald Tablet: Alchemy for Personal Transformation.* Penguin Putnam, 1999.

Larsen, Stephen. *The Mythic Imagination: The Quest for Meaning Through Personal Mythology.* Inner Traditions, 1996.

MacGregor Mathers, S. L. *The Kabbalah Unveiled.* Routledge and Kegan, 1926.

Matt, Daniel C. *The Essential Kabbalah: The Heart of Jewish Mysticism.* Harper San Francisco, 1996.

Moore, Thomas. *The Planets Within: The Astrological Psychology of Marsilio Ficino.* Studies in Jungian Thought. Bucknell University Press, 1982

Pollack, Rachel. *The Forest of Souls: A Walk Through the Tarot*. St. Paul, MN: Llewellyn, 1993.

Scholem, Gershom. *Kabbalah*. New York: Meridian, 1978.

Waite, A. E. *The Holy Kabbalah: A Study of the Secret Tradition in Israel*. London: Oracle Publishing, 1996.

_____. *The Pictorial Key to the Tarot*. New York: University Books, 1959.

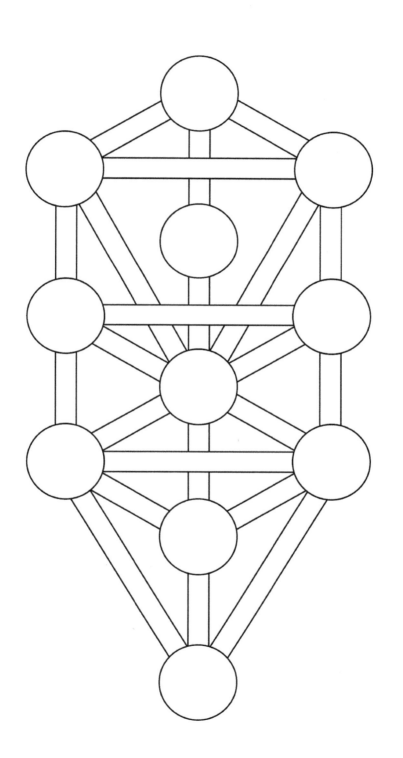

NOTES:

CPSIA information can be obtained
at www.ICGtesting.com
Printed in the USA
LVHW031512021019
632974LV00010B/873/P